MATHS
GAMES
KEY STAGE ONE
1

Shape, Space & Measures

Joe Santaniello

Published by Scholastic Ltd.,
Villiers House, Clarendon Avenue,
Leamington Spa, Warwickshire CV32 5PR
© 1995 Scholastic Ltd.

AUTHOR Joe Santaniello
EDITOR Jo Saxelby-Jennings
ASSISTANT EDITOR Joanne Boden
SERIES DESIGNER Joy White
DESIGNER Toby Long
ILLUSTRATIONS Sue Woollatt
(Graham-Cameron Illustration)
COVER ARTWORK Joy White

Designed using Aldus Pagemaker
Printed in Great Britain by Bell & Bain Ltd, Glasgow

British Library Cataloguing-in-Publication Data
A catalogue record for this book is available from the British Library.

ISBN 0-590-53360-6

Contents

Contents...

MATHS

GAMES

KEY STAGE ONE

1

Introduction

THE CONTRIBUTION OF GAMES TO TEACHING AND LEARNING

We live in a games-saturated culture. Outdoor sports and computer games are obvious examples at opposite ends of a spectrum that encompasses our everyday life. Games appeal to all sections of society, and are, therefore, levellers of difference. But games are often ephemeral. We play them, we forget them. Perhaps it is this transience which makes some teachers and parents sceptical of the value games have in learning. Games in school are often relegated to a peripheral role, as time-fillers or rewards for having completed 'important' work. The books in this series are an attempt to counterbalance this viewpoint by showing how games with clear learning objectives can be brought into the mainstream of primary teaching, to help develop key concepts and skills alongside any scheme of work.

In the context of mathematics teaching, games serve a number of educational purposes, providing an alternative forum for:
- using and applying mathematical skills and understanding;
- discussing mathematical concepts and developing mathematical language;
- developing the ability to follow instructions;
- developing co-operative learning, social and problem-solving skills;
- increasing motivation and subject interest;
- encouraging independence;
- bridging the gap between practical activities and more abstract methods of recording;
- assessing acquisition of skills and knowledge.

The games in this series of books also offer the following benefits. They:
- have clear educational objectives linked to the National Curriculum programmes of study and the Scottish 5–14 Guidelines;
- save time and money by providing photocopiable resources;
- can be adapted to suit individual needs and purposes;
- offer suggestions for differentiation;
- include game record sheets to promote data handling and record-keeping, and to provide evidence;
- have lively real-life and imaginary contexts to capture and hold the children's interest.

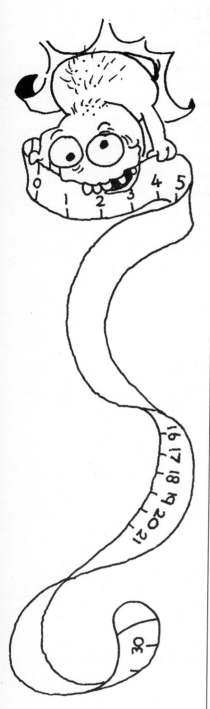

GAMES AND THE MATHEMATICS CURRICULUM

All of these games have been devised to support mathematics requirements in the National Curriculum and the Scottish 5–14 Guidelines. A vital element of many traditional games is the reinforcement of counting and number recognition skills. The games in this series build on these acknowledged benefits, extending them into less well-explored areas of the mathematics curriculum within an atmosphere of pleasurable learning. The children's imagination is captured by interlacing the mathematical content with role-playing in both 'real' and fantasy worlds. The games provide a collaborative forum for discussion and, therefore, a focus for asking questions and developing mathematical language. The decision-making, prediction and reasoning skills outlined in Using and Applying Mathematics (Attainment Target 1) are developed in all the games, and the inclusion of game record sheets ensures that data handling is integrated throughout.

THE GAMES

This book contains both non-board based games (in the section called Activity Games) as well as games that use boards and other manipulative resources (in the sections called Photocopiable Games and Special Section).

ACTIVITY GAMES

This section provides a selection of ideas for games that only require resources commonly found in classrooms. Most of the games can be played by the whole class. Some are physical activity games and are best played in a large open space such as a hall, playground or field.

PHOTOCOPIABLE GAMES

The games in this section are based on photocopiable resources that are provided. These resources include game boards (some of which have a three-dimensional element), cards, game rules, game record sheets, and playing components such as spinners and playing pieces. These games follow traditional game formats and are designed to be played in small groups. The 'make-your-own' feature of the photocopiable sheets means that games can be adapted easily and without great expense.

When making the playing pieces, cut along solid lines and fold along dotted lines.

The following symbols are used on some of the photocopiable pages:

 A calculator may be useful.

 For construction, the sheet needs to be photocopied the number of times shown.

SPECIAL SECTION

This section contains photocopiable resources to be used with games from the Photocopiable Games section. They also have wider applications for other mathematical and cross-curricular activities.

THE TEACHERS' NOTES

The teachers' notes follow a standard format for each game:

TEACHING CONTENT

The mathematical learning objectives are signposted and linked to the National Curriculum programmes of study for Key Stage One and the Scottish 5–14 Guidelines. For example: **(SSM 2a; RS: A)** indicates National Curriculum Attainment Target **S**hape, **s**pace and **m**easures: Key Stage One programme of study paragraph **2a**; Scottish 5–14 Guidelines for **S**hape, position and movement, strand **R**ange of **s**hapes, Level **A**.

WHAT YOU NEED

Resources that you will need are listed under the following headings: 'Photocopiable sheets', 'For construction' and 'For playing'.

PREPARATION

Notes are given on assembling the game and, where appropriate, suggestions made for introducing the game.

HOW TO PLAY

The aims and rules of the game are briefly summarised and any additional information for the teacher to consider is pointed out.

TEACHER'S ROLE

In some of the games the teacher is an active participant, in others a facilitator or an observer. This section helps the teacher to define her role and offers ideas for developing the game's mathematical ideas and skills. See also page 9.

GAME VARIATIONS

Where a game can be varied within the mathematical objectives set out under the 'Teaching content', ideas are given.

EXTENSION

Where a game might be extended to develop the mathematical objectives, ideas are given.

ASSESSMENT

There are three main ways that the teacher can assess the value of a game and the children's learning:

• Direct observation of the game in progress
Observation of a game allows the teacher to note how each child copes with the skills required in the game. A clipboard is handy for on-the-spot jotting down of notes. Be aware, however, that an adult presence can distort the game.

• Discussion after the game
After the game, the supervising adult can discuss what happened with the group, extending the players' horizons beyond the 'who won' mentality.

Where appropriate, pointers and suggested questions for doing this are given in the teachers' notes.

• Using game record sheets
Many games are accompanied by a game record sheet upon which the result and how it was achieved can be recorded by the players themselves, giving concrete evidence of how well they have assimilated the concept(s) behind the game. The game record sheets employ writing, drawing and data-handling skills to give the busy teacher an outline of the completed game; in many cases, these sheets can be adapted to provide differentiation for the games.

CLASSROOM MANAGEMENT

As indicated above, not all the games are board games. There are card games, pencil-and-paper games, calculator games and mental games. This variety enables the teacher to select the appropriate game for the particular classroom situation, or even for sending home to be played with parents. Group games can be played at a table or in a designated corner. Some games are suitable for individual play – a copy of a single track, for instance, can be used both as a playing surface and as a record of the game – with the child competing against himself.

THE TEACHERS' ROLE

The teachers' main task will be in the selection of the game and the setting up of play for the designated educational purpose. She will need to decide what curricular function the game can serve. It can introduce a subject; it can reinforce skills or knowledge already touched on; or it can be a means of assessment; suggestions for carrying this out are given, where appropriate, within the teachers' notes for each game.

Unless the children have played the game before, or are competent readers and can play well together on their own, the teacher (or another adult) will need to introduce and supervise the game. Ideas for introducing the games are given, where appropriate, in the teachers' notes to provide a context or stimulus for playing the game. Alternatively, the teacher can make up her own.

There is no sense in letting the children play a game and then forget it. It needs to be followed up. In the teachers' notes for each game, there are suggestions about the part the supervising adult can play in enlarging the players' horizons beyond the actual playing of the game.

Obviously, the light of experience will indicate possible variations to the games, and the photocopiable pages enable the teacher to alter details and change rules to match individual needs and purposes.

MAKING AND STORING THE GAMES

Photocopiable games are flexible and inexpensive. Even elaborate board games can be made for pence, whereas comparable commercial games could cost pounds. Also, little more than the usual art materials found in most schools is needed for their construction. So instead of having just a few games to enhance motivation and learning, the teacher can afford to be quite lavish with them.

If possible, photocopy the game boards and playing pieces directly on to card.

The appearance and motivational benefit of the games can be greatly improved by colouring them in. Felt-tipped pens are best as they don't warp the paper as much as paint. Laminating the game boards and pieces also improves appearance and increases durability.

- Making the most of parents and educational assistants

There is no reason why the teacher needs to do all the assembling. Games construction is a pleasurable activity involving colouring-in, cutting, pasting and, optionally, laminating. None of these tasks requires a teaching certificate! Parents, and even older pupils in the school, are quite capable of doing these things. Organise a games-making event involving both parents, helpers and pupils!

Similarly, a parent can be the games supervisor, instructing the group in the rules of the game, keeping an eye on its progress and conducting the discussion afterwards.

- Storing the games

Keep the various components of each game (board, pieces, game record sheets, 'How to play' sheets and so on) in a polythene bag, fastened with a wire tie. These can be attached to a 'mathematics games' board with a small bulldog clip (as shown in the illustration). Alternatively, the games can be stored in boxes – either kept individually or grouped according to difficulty in a large box and separated using coloured dividers.

ADAPTING THE GAMES

Photocopiable games are easily adapted. They can be changed to suit different purposes and abilities. You need not be stuck with a resource that only meets a small percentage of your requirements. Just delete the bit you don't want by covering with liquid paper or a sticky label, then draw and/or print your modification on top. If you are altering very fine detail, enlarge the sheet before making the alterations. Do your alterations on the enlargement, making sure to draw the lines the same density and thickness as the enlargement. Then reduce back to original size. Similarly, if a game is too big or too small, it can be altered to size using the enlarging or reducing facility on most large photocopiers. If yours can't do this, ones that can will be found in most public libraries.

Simple alterations such as writing children's names on playing pieces or using the school logo on the headings may seem small things in themselves, but they make the games more personal and special.

Copies of each adaptation can be kept in polypockets in an A4 ring binder devoted to the purpose. A slip of paper or card can be put in the pocket detailing when the adaptation was made, its curriculum focus, which class used it, notes on how effective it was and further ideas for adaptation.

CROSS-CURRICULAR CONNECTIONS

As many of the games involve role-playing and have suitable contexts to develop storylines, they fit easily into language topics. Some of the games will readily integrate with other subject areas – for example, 'Nature trail' with science and 'Treasure trek' and 'British Isles' with geography. Ideas for these, where appropriate, are offered in the 'Preparation' or 'Teacher's role' sections of the teachers' notes.

 INTRODUCTION

LINKS TO THE NATIONAL CURRICULUM

★ main game
☆ extension

Games	Programmes of Study									
	1c	2a	2b	2c	3a	3b	4a	4b	N2B	N4A
Snakes alive	★						★			
Feel the shape		★		★						
Shape detectives		★	★							
Robo walker					★					
Objects table							★	★		
Think of a number			★	★						
Right turn, left turn					★					
Shape a pattern		★								
Shape up!		★	★		★					
Magic carpet	★☆						★☆			
Shape Island		★	★							
House mouse					★					
KFS					★					
Nature trail		★			★				★	
Segment Sidney	★						★☆			
Monday's child							★			
3-D hoopla		★☆	★							
Shape dominoes		★		★						
Treasure chest					★					
Shapes railway			★							
Veggies							★			
Holdall/truckers	★☆						★☆	★☆		
Dummy				★						
What can it be?					★	★				
British Isles						★				
Right angle or 1/4 turn						★				
Fat cats	★☆						★☆	★☆		
Biker					★					
Swap over						★				
Dice towers							★			
Skeletons/nets		★	★	★						
Face to face					★					
Sym Street					★					
Treasure trek						★				
Measure, fill, weigh	★									★

LINKS TO SCOTTISH 5–14 GUIDELINES

★ main game
☆ extension

Games	Strands and attainment targets														
	ME A	ME B	ME C	ME D	RS A	RS B	RS C	PM A	PM B	PM C	PS A	PS B	RTN A	T A	S B
Snakes alive	★														
Feel the shape					★										
Shape detectives					★	★	★								
Robo walker								★	★						
Objects table	★	★													
Think of a number					★	★									
Right turn, left turn									★						
Shape a pattern					★	★									
Shape up!					★						★	★			
Magic carpet	★	☆													
Shape Island					★										
House mouse								★							
KFS								★							
Nature trail								★		★				★	
Segment Sidney	★	☆													
Monday's child														★	
3-D hoopla					★	★☆									
Shape dominoes					★	★									
Treasure chest								★							
Shapes railway					★	★									
Veggies	★														
Holdall/truckers	★	☆	☆												
Dummy					★										
What can it be?								★	★						
British Isles									★						
Right angle or 1/4 turn									★						
Fat cats	★	☆	★☆	☆											
Biker									★						
Swap over									★						
Dice towers	★	★													
Skeletons/nets					★	★	★								
Face to face															★
Sym Street															★
Treasure trek									★						
Measure, fill, weigh	★														

MATHS GAMES
KEY STAGE ONE 1

Activity games

SNAKES ALIVE

TEACHING CONTENT

★ Measuring length in context (SSM: 1c; ME: A)

★ Comparing lengths (SSM: 4a; ME: A)

PREPARATION

Cut five lengths of string or similar material, all of different length, but with at least a 10cm difference between them. Tie each length on to the handle of a bulldog clip and attach a small weight on the other end. Cut five snakes' heads from card as shown below. They should be all different colours. Draw on some features with a marker pen.

WHAT YOU NEED

String, coloured card, scissors, marker pen, bulldog clips, suitable small weights (such as balls of Plasticine), a large cardboard box or dustbin.

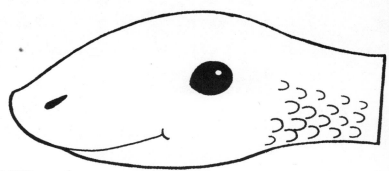

HOW TO PLAY

This is a game for two teams. One team clips the snakes' heads to the strings, without the other team seeing, and arranges the snakes in a large cardboard box or dustbin with their heads hanging over the edge. Then, without going close, the second group has to decide which snake they think is the longest. Once their choice has been made, withdraw the snakes from the box and compare them to each other. Have the children picked the longest one? The groups then swap roles and the snakes are dismantled and rearranged.

TEACHER'S ROLE

Once the children have got used to the game, show them how the snakes can be put into a rank order when being held up, with the longest at one end of the line and the shortest at the opposite end with the others ranked in between.

To give the snakes more character and to make it easier for the children to compare them, give the snakes names – use the colours or choose more adventurous names such as 'Wriggly' or 'Curly'. Begin with one-to-one comparison, using 'longer' and 'shorter' as inverses of each other. For example, if Wriggly is longer than Curly, then Curly must be shorter than Wriggly. This can be extended to comparing groups of three, and eventually four, by using one-to-one comparison and then inferring the relationship of the size of the third snake. For example, if Curly is shorter than Wriggly, to put Squiggle in position, it would have to be compared with both the other snakes. If it was compared first with Curly and found to be longer, then it would have to be compared with Wriggly too. When comparing groups of three or more the words 'longest' and 'shortest' are emphasised.

FEEL THE SHAPE

TEACHING CONTENT

☆ Identifying shapes by their edges (SSM: 2c; RS: A)
☆ Using specific words to describe shapes (SSM: 2a; RS: A)

WHAT YOU NEED

Some two-dimensional shapes, sticky labels or tape, a blindfold.

PREPARATION

Use existing commercial two-dimensional shapes or copy on to card and cut out those in the Special Section (photocopiable pages 138–139). The latter can be enlarged to a size everyone in the class can see easily. Put a 'starting point' on to each shape. This can be a folded sticky label or a piece of tape with a tiny pinch in the middle to raise it slightly from the edge, as shown below.

Ensure that the children have had experience of feeling the straight sides of some classroom objects. They must appreciate that a change in direction at a corner means the start of a new side.

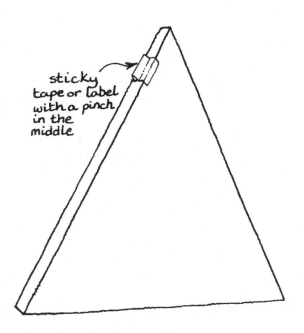

sticky tape or label with a pinch in the middle

HOW TO PLAY

This game can be played between two individuals or two teams. Lay the shapes out singly on a table. In turn, each child is blindfolded and then handed a shape by her opponent. Holding it near the starting point, the child should feel along each side, counting how many edges there are and feeling the angles. Then the player should say how many sides there are, for one point, and the shape's name, for two points. Put the shape back on the table and mix them up before the players change roles.

TEACHER'S ROLE

Concentrate initially on exploring the shapes by means of feeling round the sides and introduce the names as the children's confidence develops. Overemphasis on the names of two-dimensional shapes too early can cause confusion and obscure what a shape represents.

To introduce the correct names for the shapes, punctuate the game with short question-and-answer sessions: Does anyone know the name of this shape? Is it like any other shape we have had in the game so far? Observe how well the players are matching shape for shape, especially those shapes which are different, but have the same number of sides, such as squares, rectangles and different-shaped triangles. Extend the game by asking the children to count the angles (which the children will experience as 'corners').

In preparation for this game, or as a follow-up activity, start collections of shapes using pictures cut from magazines and newspapers and pasted on to large sheets of paper. The children can outline the basic shapes on the pictures in felt-tipped pen – squares on the sides of houses, rectangles on lorries and so on.

SHAPE DETECTIVES

TEACHING CONTENT

☆ Sorting 2-D shapes using words such as straight, curved and so on (SSM: 2a; RS: A)

☆ Looking at 3-D shapes initially as 2-D shapes (SSM: 2b; RS: B/C)

PREPARATION

This version of 'I-Spy' encourages shape identification by highlighting the characteristics of shapes. Using the immediate surroundings the players identify the characteristics of two-dimensional shapes within common objects, for example the curved edge of the circle on a clock-face or the straight edge of a square wall tile. To help the children to focus on these specific characteristics, make a set of simple word and symbol cards showing: curve, round, straight side, slope, square, square corner, bent corner. These could be integrated with the two-dimensional shape cards given in the Special Section (photocopiable pages 138–139), if they are made the same size.

HOW TO PLAY

This game is played between two individuals or teams. Start off by each player in turn asking an opposing player an 'I-Spy' question: 'I spy a shape with a curve', for example. The player gets one point for a correct answer. If the questioner denies the answer and cannot offer a credible alternative, then two points are added to the opposing team's score. Keep a tally of the teams' points.

Now introduce the word cards. The word cards are shuffled and placed face down. The first player takes the top card and, for one point, has to find that characteristic (or shape) on some object in the room or, perhaps, the playground. If the player cannot do so, the card is offered to the opposing team or player to find the characteristic, also for one point.

TEACHER'S ROLE

During the game, stress the words such as 'curve' or 'straight' and ask the children to repeat them. After the game, go through all the characteristics and get the children to identify them, drawing on examples used in the game. Ask individuals to match cards to features in the room. If you are using the cards from the Special Section, make at least four copies of each of them and the word cards, and use them to play 'Snap', 'Spread' (also called 'Pairs' or 'Pelmanism') and similar matching games.

ROBO WALKER

TEACHING CONTENT

☆ Following instructions for moving along a route (SSM: 3a; PM: B)
☆ Finding an object in the classroom (SSM: 3a; PM: A)

PREPARATION

This is a variation of 'Blind man's buff' with the 'blindfolded' person being directed along a path or through an obstacle course to a 'treasure'. The obstacles can be empty boxes from the supermarket, set at right angles to force the robot to turn, while the 'treasure' can be any object chosen by the teacher as a suitable reward. Instead of a traditional bandanna-type blindfold, the child wears a cardboard box, to look like a robot's 'head', over his own head. To make the robot's head, cover a suitable box, the right size for every player, with foil and add details such as eyes and mouth made from scrap materials covered in a different-coloured foil or painted matt black. So that it will serve as a blindfold, don't pierce the box with eye-holes.

WHAT YOU NEED

A large cardboard box, junk modelling materials, coloured foil and/or matt black paint, adhesive, suitable boxes for obstacles, a large playing space.

HOW TO PLAY

A good deal of space is needed for this game – a large room, hall or playground. Divide the class into teams. In each team, one child is the robot and then, one by one, each of the other children in the team give directions for a move forward. Directions should be given such as: 'Forward so many paces, right turn and stop, left turn and stop'. Touching an obstacle incurs penalty points. If there are a number of teams, then the team with the lowest number of penalty points wins, and the one with the highest number of points comes last.

Alternatively, the teams could start out with a set number of 'energy' points and have them deducted. This makes the game a little more intense as the robot can run out of 'energy' before completing the course. In this case, the team with the highest score wins. Once the children are familiar with the game, insist on them trying to make as few moves as possible with every instruction counting as a debit point.

TEACHER'S ROLE

Besides noting how well the children visualise forward, right and left turn, see how competent they are at anticipating the number of paces required. At this stage, further work on right and left can be expected and maze puzzles and road layouts provide natural progressions.

OBJECTS TABLE

TEACHING CONTENT

★ Comparing pairs of objects in terms of mass, length and capacity without measuring (SSM: 4a; ME: A)
★ Using scales and jugs and direct comparison of length as final checks (SSM: 4b; ME: A/B)
★ Increasing use of the vocabulary of measurement (SSM: 4a; ME: A)

PREPARATION

Fill a table with objects, both large and small containers for capacity, heavy and light objects and tall, long and short objects. Include some irregular objects, such as a skipping-rope or a funny-shaped shampoo bottle, or a deceptively light item such as a polystyrene dummy's head. In the interests of safety do not use glass items or containers that have held toxic substances. In conjunction with these objects, make a set of word cards to do with measurement, for example: longer, shorter, taller, wider, narrower, heavier, lighter, holds more, holds less, plus a few 'red herrings' such as tallest, longest, shortest, lightest and heaviest.

Talk to the children about the different words and their meanings. How often 'heaviest' and the other '-est' words will be used depends on how much the children comprehend the finer points of comparison. If you think that these words may cause confusion, they should be left out of the game. However, the children should not be allowed to use them carelessly: too often 'heaviest' is accepted when it should be 'heavier'.

WHAT YOU NEED

A variety of objects of different length, weight and capacity, a set of word cards relating to measurement – longer, holds less and so on.

HOW TO PLAY

Divide the class into two teams or arrange a knock-out competition for individuals with the winners going on to the next round.

Place the cards face down and let the players take turns to pick a card. Each player must find two objects from the table which make sense of the word card, and then show her choice to the others. If, for example, a child picks 'heavier' and then chooses a teddy bear and a shoe, the two should be put in context as: 'The teddy bear is heavier than the shoe.' The choices should be tested by weighing one object against the other. In the case of capacity, test the choices by pouring water or sand from one container into the other over a large bath. Lengths can be compared beside one another. If the choice was right, the player gains a point for her team or goes on to the next round.

TEACHER'S ROLE

After the game, talk about the words. Discuss how '-er' is used for comparing two objects and how the '-est' words are used if we mean the object with the biggest weight or the smallest length on the table. It is not an easy distinction for children to make, but by persevering an important aspect of maths is being communicated; that is, in maths words take on a special precise importance.

GAME VARIATION

The game can be expanded to include objects from around the classroom or the players can be encouraged to think of any two things which fit the word on the card: 'An elephant is heavier than a bicycle', for example. As there is no way that this can be put to the test practically let the class decide whether it is correct.

THINK OF A NUMBER

TEACHING CONTENT

☆ Associating shapes with sides, angles, faces, edges and corners (SSM: 2b and 2c; RS: A/B)

PREPARATION

Either copy on to card and cut out the two-dimensional shapes cards on photocopiable pages 138–139 and make the three-dimensional shapes from the Special Section (photocopiable pages 141–144) or use any available shapes and solids. If you are using the two-dimensional cards for a whole class game, enlarge them to A4 size so that everyone can see. The three-dimensional shapes in the Special Section do not have cards, but these can be made simply as they only need the name of the shape. If you would prefer to use picture cards for the three-dimensional shapes, copy the skeleton shapes in 'Skeletons/Nets' from the Photocopiable Games section (photocopiable page 120).

WHAT YOU NEED
Some large two- and three-dimensional shapes, paper and pencil (for scoring).

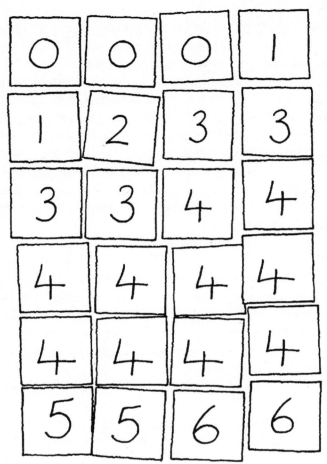

HOW TO PLAY

Allow two teams to compete against each other or have a sudden death competition for all the class, with the winners going on to the next round and the losers becoming part of the audience. All the shape cards are shuffled and placed face down in a pack. The players take turns to choose a number and call it out. The top card is turned over and the shape shown to the player and to the audience. The player then has to link his choice of number to the shape. For instance, if the child says 'four' and a square is shown, the child can say that the shape has four sides or four angles. If a triangle had been revealed, four would have been a losing choice as the child would not be able to make any links. Give one point for a correct link or allow the child to continue into the next round if they are playing as individuals. The winners are the team with the most points when everyone has had a turn or the child who made the least mistakes in her choice of number and link to the shape.

TEACHER'S ROLE

Through your selection of the shapes on the cards the game can concentrate on particular aspects of shapes. If you have been talking about the sides of shapes, you might exclude the three-dimensional shapes and concentrate solely on two-dimensional shapes. Similarly, if you have been talking about three-dimensional shapes, only the two-dimensional shapes associated with them might be kept in the pack: squares, rectangles and triangles, in the case of the shapes in the Special Section (photocopiable pages 141–144). Encourage the children to understand which of the numbers offer the most choice of links. Let the children play the game several times to see whether they begin to refine their choices of numbers. Inevitably, there will be children who just guess any number. Discuss which numbers are most useful and why. Is 3 better than 4? If not, why not? What range of numbers could be used? (This will depend on whether three-dimensional shapes have been included or not.) Ask the class to draw up a list of numbers for all the shapes and all their properties. A list of the number of faces, edges and corners for the four three-dimensional shapes in the Special Section is given in 'Dummy' on page 86 of the Photocopiable Games section.

GAME VARIATION

This game can be played in reverse with a pack of number cards (as shown above) alongside the pack of shape cards. Each player turns over the top cards in each pile and tries to make a link between them. If she can link the two, the player gains one point. The set of number cards shown apply to the two-dimensional shapes in the Special Section. The game 'Dummy' (Photocopiable Games, pages 86–88) explores the properties of the four three-dimensional shapes in the Special Section and provides a set of number cards for these. To emphasise the properties still further, instead of gaining one point for a correct link, a player could get the number on the card in points to add to her team score. Since the circle has no corners and links to the 0 card, this could have a 1 put in front making it worth ten points and giving it special status. It is the most difficult shape for the children to comprehend. In addition, look at shapes with one set or two sets of same-sized sides, for example squares and regular hexagons. If a child comes up with these in his explanation, this would be an opportunity to highlight such shapes.

RIGHT TURN, LEFT TURN

TEACHING CONTENT

☆ Practising movement forward (translation) and right or left turns (rotation) (SSM: 3a; PM: B)

PREPARATION

This game involves physically moving across a grid. The game needs a large space, such as a tarmacked playground, where you can mark out a rough grid of chalk crosses (see below).

WHAT YOU NEED

Chalk, a large tarmacked playing space, paper and pencil (for scoring).

HOW TO PLAY

In this game the class compete as two teams with each member of the team taking a turn at marching across the grid of crosses or, in the opposing team, giving the directions. Ask the teams to sit in two lines along the side of the grid. The first player stands on the first cross and his opponent calls out one of three directions: forward, right or left. Then the player has a count of three, called out by the whole class, to make a move. Each correct move to a cross counts for one point. If the player goes in the wrong direction he is out. If there is no cross in the direction called out by his opponent, the player gets another point. After gaining five points the player on the grid can 'retire' and let someone else in the team have a turn. The team with the most points when everyone has had a turn at moving and giving the directions is the winner.

TEACHER'S ROLE

During the game, observe how instinctively the children turn to the right or the left. If the class appear very hesitant, conclude with a simple game of 'Simon says', concentrating on right and left: 'Left hand up, Simon says left hand up, right foot forward, Simon says right foot forward' and so on.

SHAPE A PATTERN

TEACHING CONTENT

☆ Describing and discussing shapes and patterns that can be seen or visualised (SSM: 2a; RS: A/B)

PREPARATION

Two identical sets of shapes are needed; one set for each team. The range and number of shapes, as well as the complexity of the game, will be determined by the teaching needs identified for the particular group playing. The shapes can be commercially-produced classroom resources, or sets made up from the shapes in the Special Section (photocopiable pages 138–144). They can be sets of two-dimensional shapes or three-

WHAT YOU NEED

A large playing space such as the hall or playground, two identical sets of shapes (see 'Preparation'), paper and pencil (for scoring).

dimensional shapes or a mixture, and could include different-sized examples of each shape (for example, a big circle and a little circle) and more than one of each.

HOW TO PLAY

Divide the children into two equal teams and tell them to line up, one behind the other, in their teams at one end of the hall. Place the two sets of shapes in separate piles at the other end of the hall. Describe out loud a pattern of shapes – for example, 'Circle, rectangle, triangle', or 'Four-sided shape, three-sided shape, a shape with one curved side.' The first player on each team should run to their respective pile of shapes, pick out the relevant ones and place them in the order you called out. They then run back to the end of their line. The first player to return to their team having made the correct pattern wins a point for the team. Repeat this, giving a different pattern each time, until all the players have had a go. At the end of the playing time, the team with the most points wins.

TEACHER'S ROLE

As well as choosing the set of shapes to be used, appropriate to the ability of the group playing, you can also determine the complexity of the patterns to be made and of the descriptions you give. Although memory is not a particular skill being developed here, you could increase the number of shapes in the pattern, or require that the pattern you give be repeated a certain number of times. You could describe a shape by number of sides, faces, edges or angles. The variations are numerous!

As only two children are playing at any one time, you should be able to observe those that are having difficulty relating the shapes to your descriptions. During play, ask the children if they can describe individual shapes and/or patterns in different ways. For example, if you had described a circle as a 'round' shape, the children might say you could also describe it as 'a circle', 'a shape with no straight sides', 'a shape with no angles' and so on. Try to elicit as many different descriptions as you can for each shape. Can the children fit more than one shape to a particular description?

SHAPE UP!

TEACHING CONTENT

☆ Recognising and matching 2-D shapes (SSM: 2a; RS: A)
☆ Drawing simple 2-D shapes (SSM: 2b; RS: A)
☆ Making, copying and continuing patterns (SSM: 3a; PS: A/B)

PREPARATION

Make a large shapes dice by sticking a different cardboard shape on to each face of a play brick: circle, triangle, square, rectangle, pentagon and hexagon. The children will enjoy the novelty of using a plant pot 'shaker'.

HOW TO PLAY

This is an outdoor game for two teams, the object of which is to be the

WHAT YOU NEED

A large tarmacked playing space, two pieces of chalk, a large play brick, card, a black felt-tipped pen, scissors, adhesive, a plant pot.

first to copy a sequence of four shapes a set number of times.

The teams create their own shapes sequence by taking it in turns to 'throw' the dice four times each. For example, Team A might throw a circle, then a pentagon, then a triangle and finally a hexagon. They draw this pattern with chalk on the ground. Team B might throw a triangle, then a rectangle, then a circle and then another triangle. They also chalk their pattern on the ground.

The game continues with the members of the teams taking turns to throw the dice and trying to repeat their pattern the number of times set. So Team A must first throw a circle, then a pentagon, and so on. Each time a throw is successful, that shape is chalked on the ground to continue the pattern. The first team to complete their pattern is the winner.

TEACHER'S ROLE

You will need to determine the number of times the pattern is to be repeated. It should be sufficient to allow each member of a team to have at least one go at throwing the dice. At the end of the game, draw the children's attention to the overall patterns they have created. For example, because Team B's initial sequence had a triangle at the beginning and the end, the continued pattern will have two triangles next to each other. It is also possible, with an initial sequence of four shapes, that there will be repetition within that sequence (for example, triangle, circle, triangle, circle).

GAME VARIATIONS

• The game can be varied not only by varying the number of times the initial sequence is repeated, but also by varying the number of shapes in the initial sequence. You could also choose to use other two-dimensional shapes.

• The game could also be played on a smaller scale indoors, with two to four players using pencils and paper.

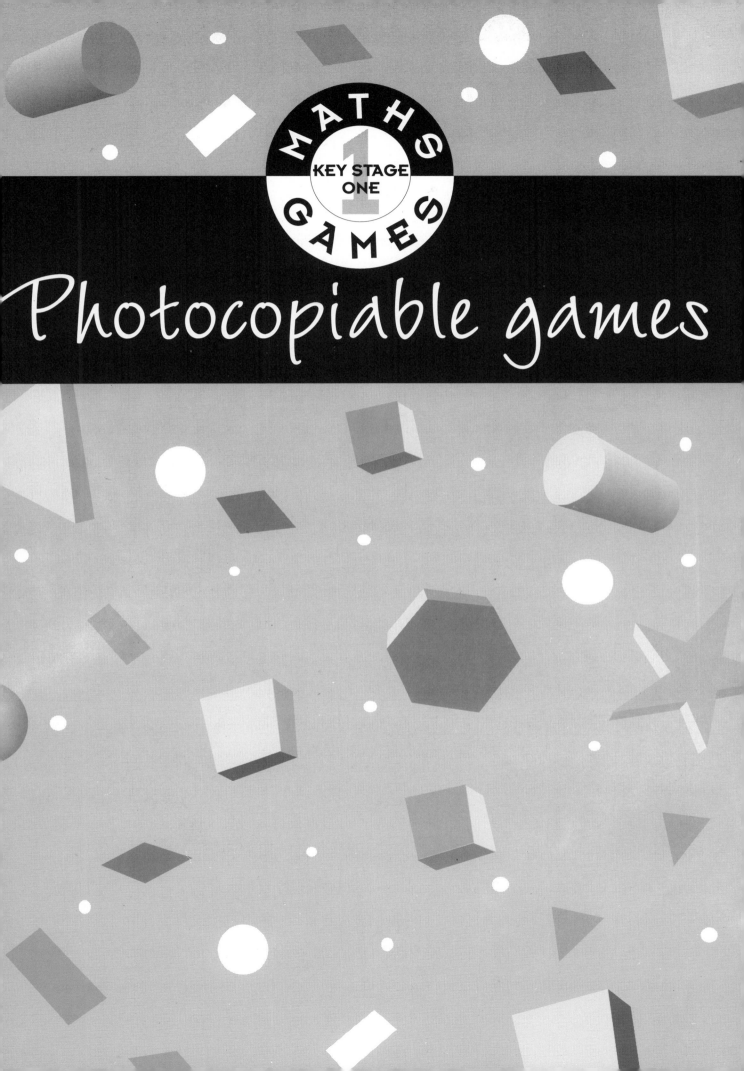

MATHS GAMES

KEY STAGE ONE

1

Photocopiable games

MAGIC CARPET

TEACHING CONTENT

★ Measuring lengths in practical contexts (SSM: 1c; ME: A)
★ Comparing and estimating lengths (SSM: 4a; ME: A)

PREPARATION

Assembling the game: The magic carpet (page 29), the different lengths and the stand-up cuddly toys (page 30) are best copied directly on to card. Cut out, colour and assemble the stand-up figures. The lengths are identified by their dice numbers and their patterns which can be coloured to match the magic carpet itself. However, on no account colour in the blank lengths on the game board, so that they will be seen by the children as spaces. The fact that the animals can be moved around from corner to corner, allows a variety of lengths between them and demonstrates that the positions of the figures do not determine the lengths of the lines.

Introducing the game: Tell the children that the cuddly toys found this magic carpet. Each of them sat down near a corner of the carpet – which were the right places for the magic to lift them into the sky – but the magic carpet didn't work! In order for it to fly, the carpet must be complete. The six empty spaces between the friends must be filled with magic lengths woven with flying spells. Only when the magic pattern on the carpet has been finished, will the carpet rise into the air and carry the toys off to new adventures. But only the right length fits the right place on the mat. Can the children help the cuddly toys to fit the magic lengths on to the carpet and complete the magic pattern?

HOW TO PLAY

This is a very simple game for two to four players. In turn, the players throw the dice and pick up the length that matches the number thrown and place it in position on the magic carpet. If the length has already been put in place, that player can do nothing and play passes on to the next player. The player who puts the last length in place wins.

This is rather a quick game, but time could be spent afterwards sticking down the lengths or completing the record sheet (page 31) by mapping the animals to the lengths (see below).

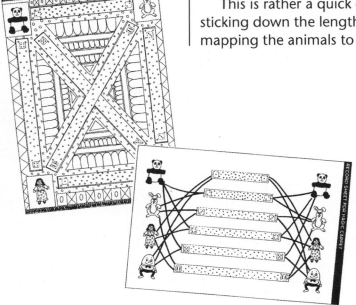

TEACHER'S ROLE

Help the children in the post-game recording. Discuss with them whether it makes any difference to the lengths which cuddly toy is on which corner. Although the lengths fit the same positions on the carpet, irrespective of which cuddly toys are placed where, most children will not appreciate this at first. When and if they do, although it means they can match the lengths more easily during the game, it does show their understanding of the different lengths and their relative positions.

WHAT YOU NEED

PHOTOCOPIABLE PAGES

Magic carpet sheet 29, playing pieces (lengths and stand-up cuddly toys) sheet 30, record sheet 31, 'How to play' sheet 28.

FOR CONSTRUCTION

Card, scissors, adhesive, coloured crayons or pens.

FOR PLAYING

Magic carpet baseboard, a set of paper lengths, a 'How to play' sheet, a dice and shaker.

This is an opportunity to introduce the vocabulary 'nearest' and 'furthest away', linking it to the numbered lengths. Start with a specific animal: Which toy is nearest to the panda? Which is furthest away? How can we tell? Let's measure and see. Move on to more general relationships: Which two animals are nearest together? How can we tell? (By comparing the lengths of the strips.) Which two are furthest away?

GAME VARIATIONS

• A longer game will result if every player has his own magic carpet game board to fill in. Remember that you will need a full set of lengths available for each player in the middle at the start.

• In this version, the board becomes the record sheet, as well as the playing surface. Using the stick-on animals, a number of layouts can be copied before the game is used. Copy the animals a few times, cut them out and recopy them until you have an A4 master of the stick-on animals. Make a number of copies of the carpet layout and stick the animals in the corners in a variety of permutations; top left rabbit for one, top left panda for another, top left Humpty for another and so on, for all four corners as shown below. Make copies of these layouts as masters for future reference or for use with other members of the class. Give them to the children uncoloured. As before, the children use the paper lengths for the game. Afterwards, the lengths can be stuck down completing the magic pattern. Finally, when dry, the whole sheet can be coloured in and used as a stepping off point for follow-up work.

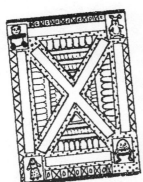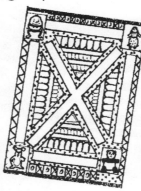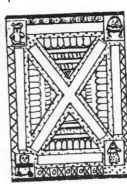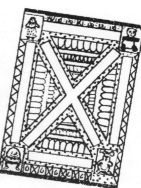

EXTENSION

☆ Measuring in practical contexts (SSM: 1c; ME: B)
☆ Comparing and estimating lengths (SSM: 4a; ME: B)
☆ Using 'centimetre' and 'cm' (SSM: 4a; ME: B)

Give each player his own individual magic carpet game board and a complete set of lengths and a record strip (photocopiable sheet 32). As before, scatter all the lengths in the middle. Then tell the players to take turns to throw the dice and take the corresponding length, until one player finishes his carpet. Stop the game at this point, with everyone having varying numbers of lengths. Help the children to complete their record strips, by measuring their lengths with a centimetre ruler and then filling in the number sentence on the record strip. There will be only one complete sentence; that of the winning child who has collected all six lengths. The other game positions are determined as second longest, third longest and so on. Show how each child's addition sentence on the record strip can be checked against a centimetre-marked metre stick by simply lining up the strips alongside it.

HOW TO PLAY MAGIC CARPET

For 2 to 4 players

YOU NEED: the magic carpet, the six lengths, cuddly toys playing pieces, a dice and a shaker.

❶ Put the cuddly toys on the magic carpet and scatter the lengths beside it.

❷ Take turns to throw the dice and pick up the length with that number on and put it on the carpet.

❸ If the length has already been used, play goes on to the next player.

❹ The player who puts the last length on the carpet is the winner.

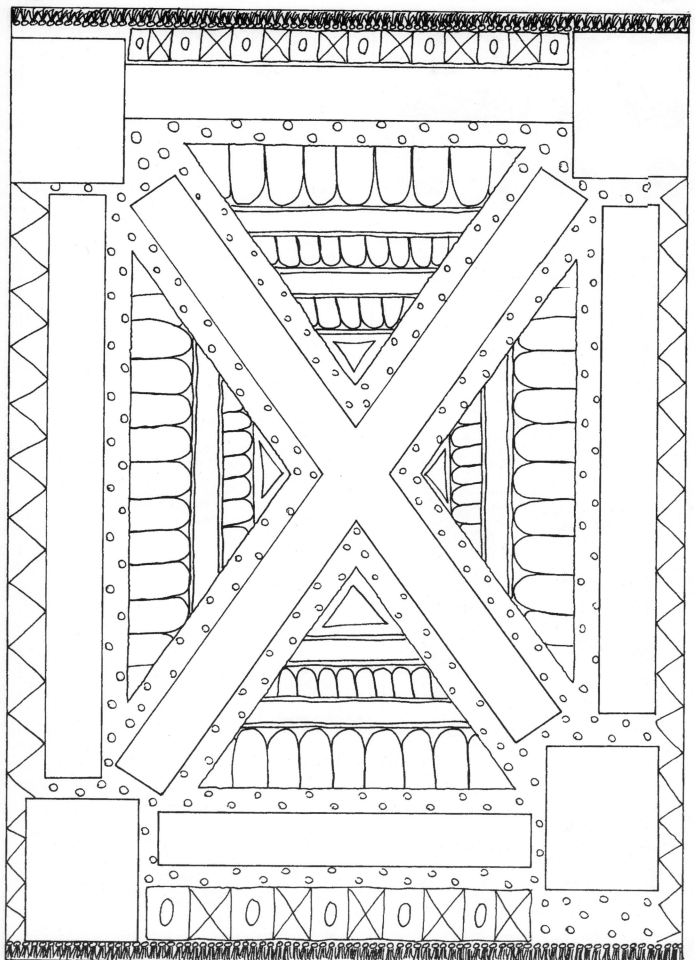

PLAYING PIECES

RECORD SHEET FOR MAGIC CARPET

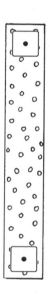

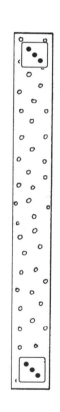
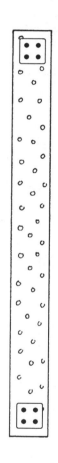
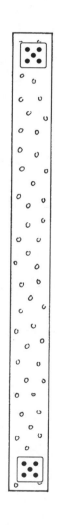

RECORD SHEET FOR MAGIC CARPET (EXTENSION)

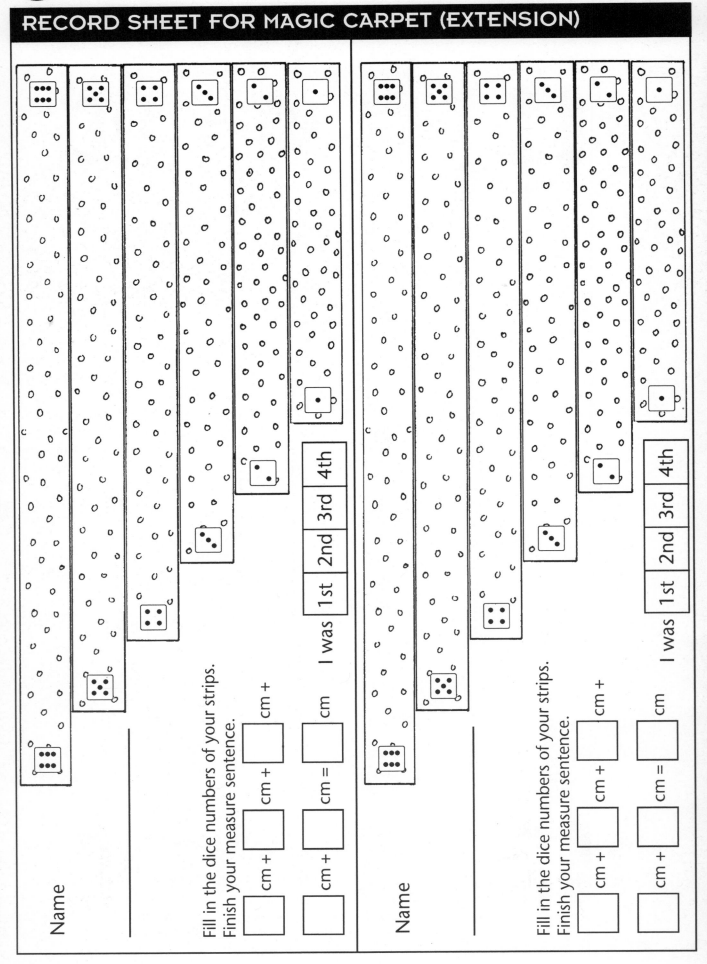

Name

Fill in the dice numbers of your strips.
Finish your measure sentence.

[ ] cm + [ ] cm + [ ] cm +
[ ] cm + [ ] cm = [ ] cm

I was | 1st | 2nd | 3rd | 4th

Name

Fill in the dice numbers of your strips.
Finish your measure sentence.

[ ] cm + [ ] cm + [ ] cm +
[ ] cm + [ ] cm = [ ] cm

I was | 1st | 2nd | 3rd | 4th

SHAPE ISLAND

TEACHING CONTENT

☆ Visualising shapes that fit into similar-shaped spaces (SSM: 2a; RS: A)
☆ Seeing the differences between shapes and beginning to categorise them (SSM: 2b; RS: A)

PREPARATION

Assembling the game: Photocopy the island section (photocopiable page 36) six times and arrange them as a hexagon and mount them on to a board about 45cm across, as shown on the record sheet. Cut the board to shape and colour the island in green, the water in blue and the sandy bank in yellow. The shape spaces are best left uncoloured to draw attention to them. The shape 'stepping-stones' should be coloured in brown and also mounted on to card. You will need six sets of them and, during play, they should be kept together in a tray to be passed from player to player. A spinner is used to identify the shapes. Mount the spinner on to card, with a sharp pencil or similar as the pivot. A dab of PVA adhesive above and below the junction with the spinner will help to hold it in place. The record sheet is an optional extra.

Introducing the game: Before the game, let the children experiment with the spinner. Make sure that they can match a shape in the game to a shape on the spinner. Talk excitedly about how there are special stepping-stones in magical shapes to help them to get to Shape Island. Discuss the function of stepping stones. There may be a variety of ideas, but here it is because the edge of the island is wet and marshy and the stones will stop them getting their feet wet. Encourage the children to look closely at the shapes: What's this shape, and this shape? Explain that to get to the island they will have to put the stones down in the right order: Which stone do we need to begin with? What comes next, and next? Which stone is on the island?

HOW TO PLAY

Each of the six players select a section of the board on which to play. They should then take turns to spin the spinner and see if it matches the shape that they require. The stepping-stones must be put down in the right order, so the first stepping-stone needs a circle, the second needs a rectangle, and so on. Shapes spun out of sequence do not count and play passes on to the next player. The player who gets the triangle on the island first is the winner. Play continues until all the other players have reached the island. To add extra interest to the game, the children could use favourite figurines, such as toy animals, to 'step' on to each stone as it is collected.

TEACHER'S ROLE

This game introduces the circle, square, rectangle and triangle in a more formal way than the children may have known them previously. The names and numbers have been put on the sheet as an aid for those children who are trying to read everything, and to reinforce the sequence of stepping stones. However, if these are inappropriate, delete them and rely on the shapes of the empty spaces.

After the game, talk more about the shapes using the two-dimensional shapes from the Special Section (photocopiable pages 138–139) or the record sheet (photocopiable page 37). See if the children can match the shapes they have used in the game with the cards. Ask them how they are the same and how they are different.

If the children are a little more advanced, write each player's name in the box under a segment of the record sheet and give them each a special colour. Instead of all the players continuing to the end, end the game immediately one player gets to the island. Then encourage all the players to colour in on the record sheet the stepping-stones they went on. Discuss how many shapes they each 'stepped' on and how many were left, what shapes they got and what shapes they wanted, how many 'stepping-stones' they collected altogether and how many were left.

GAME VARIATIONS

• Make a dice to use instead of the spinner by sticking the appropriate shapes on to a plastic cube with the two blank faces having 'Miss a turn', or even 'Put back your last shape', to give a more complex game.

• If the players wander from their own sections on to others, use a colour-coded version of the game. Colour in the sets of stones and the corresponding empty spaces on the board in six different colours.

HOW TO PLAY SHAPE ISLAND

For 2 to 6 players

YOU NEED: the Shape Island game board, six sets of shapes 'stepping-stones' in a tray and the shapes spinner.

❶ Sort out the playing order.

❷ Take turns to spin the spinner. It has to show the same shape as the first stepping stone, a circle, for you to start. Any other shape, and play passes on to the next player.

❸ You must put down the stepping stones in the right order.

❹ The player who gets to the island first is the winner.

❺ Continue playing to find who is 2nd, 3rd, 4th, 5th and 6th.

SPINNER

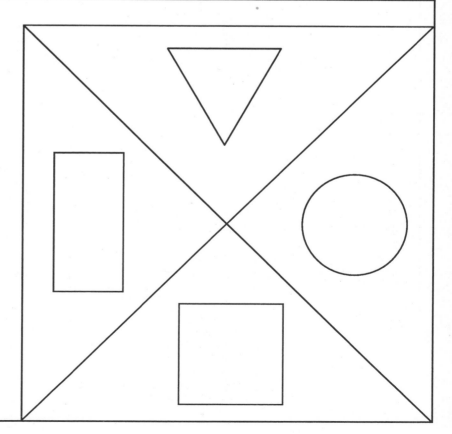

SHAPE ISLAND GAME BOARD & PLAYING PIECES

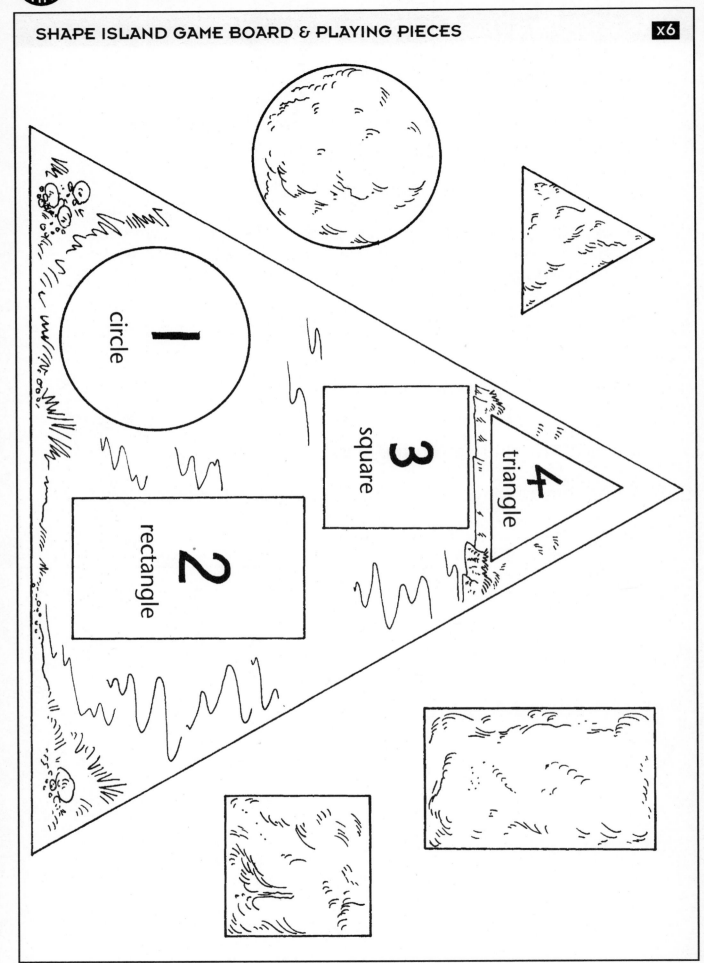

circle

1

rectangle

2

square

3

triangle

4

RECORD SHEET FOR SHAPE ISLAND

HOUSE MOUSE

HOUSE MOUSE

TEACHING CONTENT

☆ Using common words to describe location (SSM: 3a; PM: A)
☆ Using three dimensions to locate positions (SSM: 3a; PM: A)
☆ Showing locations by means of arrows, pictures and words
   (SSM: 3a; PM: A)

PREPARATION

Assembling the game: Construct the mouse 'house' from a suitable box, such as a shoebox, with two sides cut away, or from a folded strip of card stapled down on to a thick card base. It should be about 20cm square. Cut out a doorway and a mouse hole. Copy the furniture (pages 40 and 41) directly on to card. It is easily assembled if the flaps are held with paper clips while the adhesive is drying. If the furniture is to be coloured, do this before cutting out and gluing. The items have no particular positions in the house except that the clock should be stuck on to a wall. The position cards (on page 42) are best copied directly on to card also. If you decide to produce more than one set (in order to potentially lengthen the game), only keep one 'cat' card in the pack.

Introducing the game: Drawing on cartoon characters, such as Tom and Jerry, and the children's experience of their pets, talk about how cats chase mice. Show the children the mouse 'house' and the mouse playing piece. Explain how the mouse is in the habit of sneaking in to explore, but it gets scared. It knows there is a cat in the house and has to get out before the cat comes into the room.

HOW TO PLAY

This game is an abstract form of 'Hide-and-seek' for any small number of players. Start by setting up the furniture in the house and shuffling the cards. Each player in turn takes the top card and puts the mouse playing piece where the card says. The rest of the group monitor that it has been placed correctly, pointing out and correcting any obvious mistakes. The used card is left face up in a second pile which will not be used again in this game. The winner is the player who puts the mouse *through* the doorway or the mouse hole. If the cat card is turned up before this happens, the game ends as the cat has got the mouse!

TEACHER'S ROLE

After the game, go over some of the places the mouse could and should not go. For example, why is inside a television not a good idea? Use this discussion to remind the children about the dangers of electricity. The poor mouse might get electrocuted! One advantage of this game is that the mouse can be put inside things. Use this facility to the full.

GAME VARIATION

This game could be played in a large-scale follow-up version. Tell each child in the class to make a card with a direction word, a drawing and an arrow relating to the classroom and its fittings. Then ask one child to act the part of the mouse and go where the cards direct. There could even be a 'cat' waiting to catch the 'mouse', if a cat card were included.

WHAT YOU NEED

PHOTOCOPIABLE PAGES
Furniture sheets 40 and 41, 'How to play' sheet 39, position cards sheet 42.

FOR CONSTRUCTION
Scissors, adhesive, coloured crayons or pens, a shoebox or thick card and staple gun.

FOR PLAYING
Mouse 'house' and furniture, 'How to play' sheet, mouse playing piece, position cards.

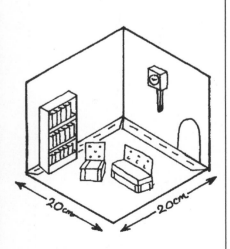

Setting up the mouse house

HOW TO PLAY HOUSE MOUSE

For 2 or more players

YOU NEED: the mouse house and furniture, the mouse playing piece, the position cards.

❶ Set up the furniture in the mouse house.

❷ Shuffle the cards and place them face down in the centre.

❸ Take turns to turn over the top card.

❹ Each time put the mouse where the card shows. Then leave the used card in a face up pile.

❺ If a 'through' card is turned over, the mouse escapes and the player who turned it over is the winner. If the cat card is shown, the game ends. Everyone has lost!

MOUSE HOUSE FURNITURE

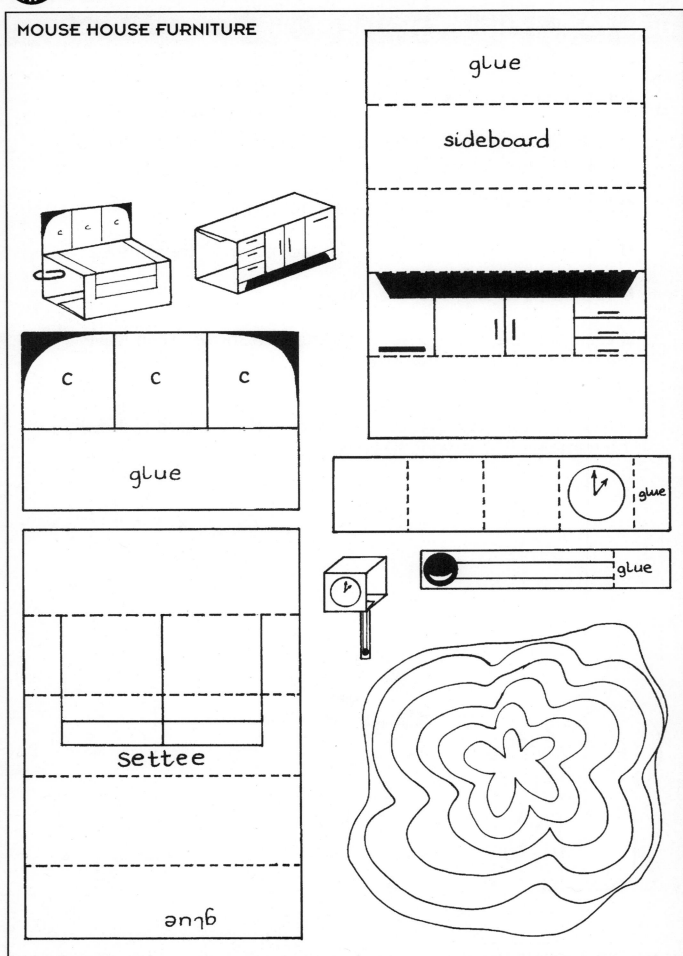

glue

sideboard

glue

c   c   c

glue

glue

glue

settee

ǝnꞁƃ

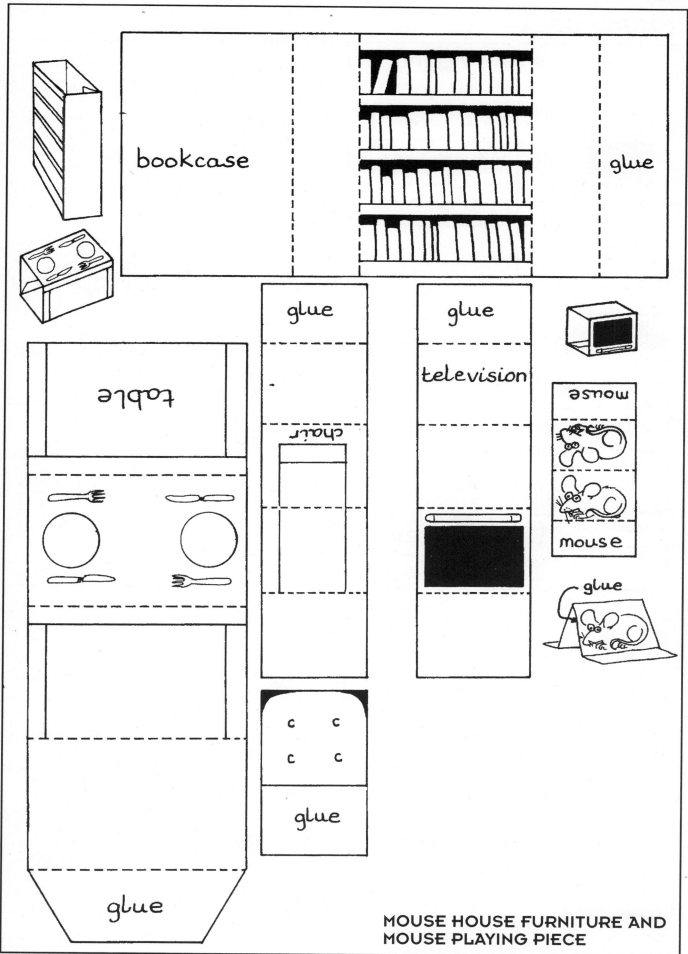

bookcase

glue

table

glue

glue

television

chair

mouse

mouse

glue

c c

c c

glue

glue

**MOUSE HOUSE FURNITURE AND
MOUSE PLAYING PIECE**

POSITION CARDS

KFS

WHAT YOU NEED

PHOTOCOPIABLE PAGES
*Table mat sheet 45, cutlery sheet
46, 'How to play' sheet 44.*
FOR CONSTRUCTION
*Coloured card or coloured pens
or crayons, scissors.*
FOR PLAYING
*A table mat, plate, glass and set
of cutlery for each player, a tray,
a dice and shaker.*

TEACHING CONTENT

☆ Practising simple position names: right, left, above, below
(SSM: 3a; PM: A)
☆ Practising the pattern and position of cutlery, plate and glass for a
meal (SSM: 3a; PM: A)

PREPARATION

Assembling the game: Copy the table mat on to paper, or card if a more
durable 'mat' is desired. The knife, fork, spoon, plate and glass cards are
best copied directly on to card. Curve the 'glass' round and staple or glue
it into a tube shape. You will need a full set of KFS cards, including a glass,
and a mat for each player. A tray to hold the various items is useful and
enhances the game's appearance. Each set of cards and mat could be
coloured in a matching colour or copied on to the same coloured card.

Introducing the game: Before the game, discuss laying the table. It must
be appreciated that not every family does this, or even if they do, they do
not necessarily lay the items in the same order. Instead of presenting the
game as the 'right' way to do things, and perhaps alienating the home,
introduce the game as laying the table for a café or restaurant where the
players are the waiters and waitresses. The waiter or waitress who finishes
first not only wins, but also gets an extra treat.

HOW TO PLAY

Each player throws the dice in turn and takes the item of cutlery, plate or
glass with the same number. If the player already has that item, she can
do nothing and play passes on to the next player. If the player rolls a 6,
play also passes on to the next player. The first player to get a full
table mat is the winner. Play goes on until everyone has a
complete table mat.

TEACHER'S ROLE

During the game, the children should be able to match the
various items to the table mat. To some extent the group will be
self-regulating, as those playing will be quick to point out each
other's mistakes. When the game has ended, ask the winner what
kind of treat he would like if he worked in a café – free ice-cream,
perhaps? Move on to build upon the children's experience to
demonstrate right and left, above and below. Use the plate as a
reference point for questions such as: What is to the *right* of the
plate? Hold up your *right* hands. What is to the *left* of the plate?
Hold up your *left* hands. What is *above* the plate? Point to
something *above* your mouth.

Integrate this game with setting up a class café complete with
waiters and waitresses, a cook and customers, money and a till.
Use imitation food that the children have made themselves with
Plasticine, or baked and painted flour and water dough, or tissue
paper. Stress to the children that this 'food' should not be eaten,
to prevent any upset tummies.

HOW TO PLAY KFS

For 2 to 4 players

YOU NEED: a tray, a table mat and a set of KFS cards, with a 'glass', for each player, a dice and a shaker.

❶ Put the glasses, cutlery and plate cards on a tray on the table. Make sure that each player has a table mat.

❷ Take turns to throw the dice and take an item for your table mat with the same number.

❸ If you already have that item for your mat, play passes to the next player. If you throw a 6, play also passes to the next player.

❹ The first player to get a full mat is the winner.

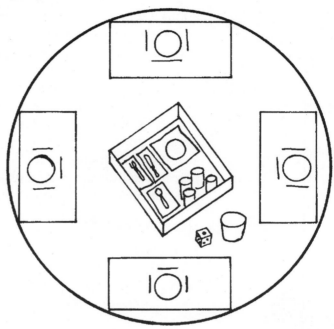

KFS TABLE MAT GAME BOARD

KFS TABLE MAT GAME BOARD

glue, tape or staple

KFS PLATE, CUTLERY AND 'GLASS' CARDS

NATURE TRAIL

TEACHING CONTENT

★ Gaining experience in moving along a route (SSM: 3a; PM: A)
★ Associating position with a sequence of objects (SSM: 3a; PM: A)
★ Converting an irregular line into a symbolic straight line (record sheet) (SSM: 2a; PM: C)
★ Expressing the orderly sequence of events in ordinal numbers (N: 2b; RTN: A)

PREPARATION

Assembling the game: Mount the game board (page 50) on to thick card. Mount or photocopy one copy of record sheet 51 directly on to thin card. Cut out the animal discs and discard the rest of the sheet. The players can choose a path on the game board by using either the three-path spinner or a dice with opposite pairs of faces covered with each of the three path designs. Copy or mount the spinner (given on sheet 49) on to thin card and push a sharp pencil through the middle. The spinner can be held in place with a dab of PVA adhesive above and below the junction with the pencil. Emphasise the differences between the paths by colouring them in distinct colours on the game board and on the dice/spinner, for example yellow, brown and red.

Introducing the game: This game could be used as part of a wider-ranging topic about country parks and woodlands, including bark rubbings and leaf and seed collections. Before the game, discuss the 12 animals shown on the discs. Draw attention to their names and habitats. Explain that the first player to 'observe' four animals along their chosen path will be the winner. Which animals do they think they will see?

HOW TO PLAY

This is a game for three players. Shuffle the animal discs and place them face down on the game board, one on each circle. Each player chooses a path and then takes it in turn to spin the spinner (or throw the dice) to give a path. Whichever player is on that path can turn over her next disc. The first player to turn over all her discs is the winner. Continue playing to find out who will be second and third.

The record sheet provides a simple group mapping exercise. It can be filled in during the game to plot progress or at the end as a record of the routes. There are several ways in which this sheet can be completed.

• Give each child a different coloured pen. Tell them to join each animal they 'see' to the circle on their path on the record sheet on which it occurred. While the result may look quite messy, it enables children who would have difficulty with reading numbers or letters to record a result.

• Each animal has a letter beside it. Tell the children to write the correct letter into each circle on their path on the record sheet.

• You may wish to adapt the record sheet by writing, or asking the children to write, 1, 2, 3, 4, or 1st, 2nd, 3rd and 4th, in the circles on the paths and then ask the children to join the circles back to the appropriate animals. Encourage them by asking questions such as: What animal did you 'see' first on your path? Which was the third animal on the cobbled/brick/paved path?

TEACHER'S ROLE

Ask the children if they can remember each animal's name as the discs are turned over: What animal is this? What does it eat? Encourage them to identify the animal's position on the path. Is it first, second, third or fourth? Watch out for any difficulties the children might have with determining the next circle; that is, with forward movement along a route. If the record sheet is used observe how well the players correlate their position on the game board with the sequence of circles on the sheet. The conversion of the irregular path to the straight line on the record sheet is an early introduction to symbolic representation, as on a motorway diagram or the London underground map, for example. Neither map bears any relation to reality other than ordinal order.

GAME VARIATIONS

• This game can be lengthened by the players only moving along the path if they spin their own path. For any other path they do nothing and play passes to the next player.

• 'Nature trail' can also be played as a paper and pencil (coloured pens) game as a resource for the whole class. Photocopy the record sheet and the game board an equal number of times. Cut out the animal discs and stick them on to the game boards, varying the order and types of animals (see illustration below). Over a hundred different layouts are possible, with no two games the same. Have copies of these sheets available for groups of three children to choose from and complete. The game is played as on the board, but instead of turning over the animal discs, the players colour in the animals along their path. In this way the layout becomes a record of the game.

HOW TO PLAY NATURE TRAIL

For 3 players only

YOU NEED: the Nature trail game board, the spinner and the 12 animal discs.

❶ Shuffle the discs and place one face down on each of the circles along the paths.

❷ Pick a path each, then take turns to spin the spinner.

❸ When it lands it shows a path. The player on that path can move on to his or her next disc and turn it over.

❹ The first player to turn over all four of their discs is the winner.

❺ Carry on playing to see who will be in second and third places. Then complete the record sheet.

SPINNER

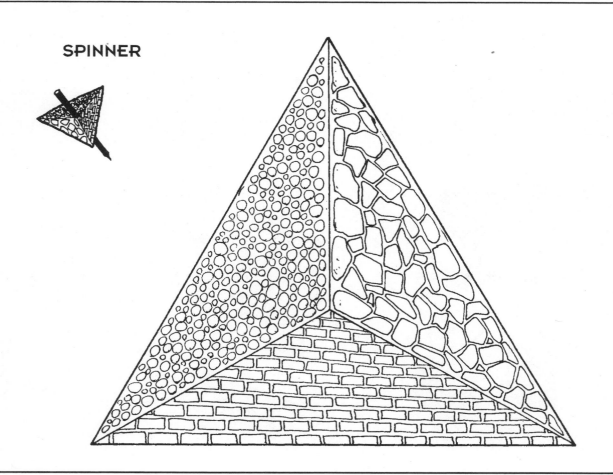

GROUP RECORD SHEET FOR NATURE TRAIL

x2

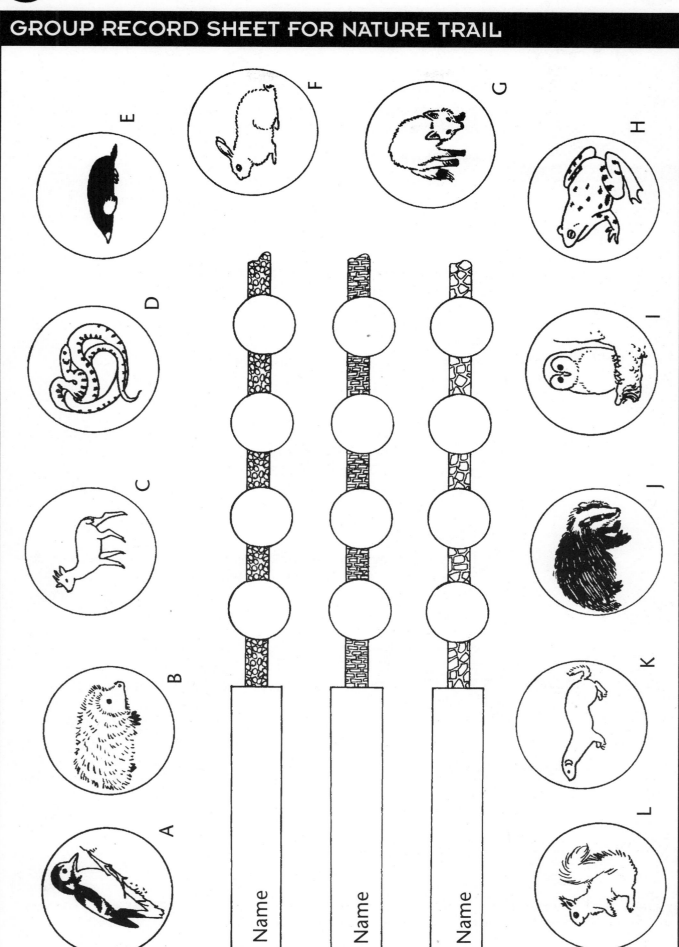

Name

Name

Name

SEGMENT SIDNEY

TEACHING CONTENT

☆ Comparing and estimating non-standard lengths (SSM: 4a; ME: A)
☆ Using a real-life context for measuring (SSM: 1c; ME: A)

PREPARATION

Assembling the game: You will need to allow at least one complete 'Segment Sidney' caterpillar per player; two are given on the photocopiable sheet (page 55). Cut out and decorate the segments, if you wish, and then stick them individually. Secure each one with a paper clip until they are dry. Or staple them near to the bottom of the segment. This also gives a little extra 'weight'. However, you will need to put sticky tape over the staple tacks to protect the children's fingers.

Introducing the game: Before starting the game, introduce Segment Sidney. Explain that 'segment' means 'a part' and discuss other things that are divided into many similar parts, such as the slices in a sliced loaf of bread or the squares of a chocolate bar.

HOW TO PLAY

Any number can play this game, making caterpillars of any length. Let each player select a head and a tail, then put the rest of the segments in the centre of play. The players then take turns to throw the dice and pick up the number of segments shown on the dice. Play continues until all the segments have been taken. An exact number must be thrown to claim the last segment(s).

TEACHER'S ROLE

This game focuses on comparative length by using stand-up caterpillar segment cards. When all the players have constructed their caterpillars, observe how the children compare them. Do they stand them side-by-side or do they count the number of segments? Ask the children to measure objects in the room in terms of caterpillar segments, for instance, a book may be one caterpillar with head, tail and six segments.

A more permanent record of the children's stand-up caterpillars can be made by running off extra copies of the photocopiable sheet and cutting each caterpillar strip in half lengthways (which will give four half caterpillars). Give each player a half caterpillar to cut up into segments. Then help the children to stick the same number of flat segments as there are stand-up segments in their 'Sidney' on to thin strips of paper. Write the children's names on to the strips

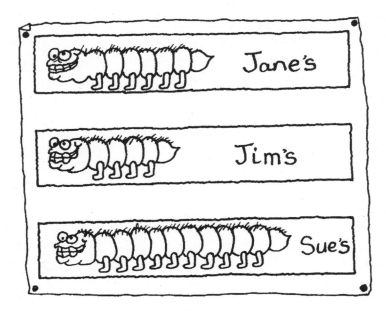

and when dry, let them decorate their flat caterpillars as they wish. Encourage them to use a variety of colours and patterns. Any patterns on the stand-up caterpillars could be copied exactly so that the players can see which segments were used in each individual caterpillar. Mount the completed flat caterpillars one above the other in a block graph formation so that the longest and shortest stand-up caterpillars in the whole class can be determined (see illustration on page 52).

GAME VARIATION

Instead of making individual Segment Sidneys, the group could make a monster one. Use only one head and tail, but supply lots of legs in the centre of play. As before, the players should select the number of segments according to the roll of the dice. The player who puts the last segment in place wins. Again, an exact number must be thrown for the last segment.

EXTENSION

☆ Comparing and estimating standard lengths (SSM: 4a; ME: B)
☆ Introducing 'centimetres' and 'metres' and 'cm' and 'm' (SSM: 4a; ME: B)

Each 'Sidney' segment, including the head and tail, is 2.5cm long. Therefore, it is relatively simple to link the caterpillars to standard metre, or fractions of a metre, lengths. The caterpillars on the sheet are 25cm, or 0.25m long. The children could play games making 0.5m or even 1m caterpillars by working in pairs. Remember that for each additional 0.25m, the children will need 25 extra body segments – a full Segment Sidney and one extra for the group to share (to make up for the discarded second head and tail segments). Play the game as before, but encourage the children to fill in the record sheet (photocopiable page 56) at the end. If the group is bigger than four, it may be better to cut up the record sheets into individual strips; one for each player. The record sheet requires the players to see how many pairs of legs their caterpillars have, reinforcing patterns of two, and then to make a simple calculator check of their own counting. This requires the children to understand halves of a length not just as a vulgar fraction, but as a decimal. A calculator is necessary. Suggest to the group that they check their work by lining up their caterpillars alongside a metre stick (or two if the group is more than four).

To investigate particular fractions of a metre provide each player with a 'mat' 3cm wide and the length of the fraction to be investigated cut from thick coloured paper or card. A different colour for each of the four would be attractive and helpful for post-game discussion. As before, the players should choose segments according to the throw of the dice. However, towards the end of the game the exact number must be thrown to fit the last few segments in place on the mat. Ask those players who did not complete their caterpillar/mat match 'How many segments did you need to fill the mat?' As the segments are a fraction number, that is 2.5cm or 2½cm, this takes a little more thought than just measuring the gap and dividing by 2.

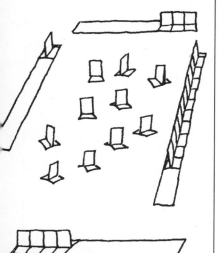

As in the original game variation, a group could make a monster caterpillar and measure it. Have a 'monster' competition between groups to see who can get the biggest caterpillar (measure its exact length in centimetres) in a limited number of throws.

HOW TO PLAY SEGMENT SIDNEY

For 2 or more players

YOU NEED: at least one complete Segment Sidney per player, a dice and shaker.

❶ You will need a head and a tail segment each.

❷ Place the rest of the segments in the middle of the table.

❸ Take turns to throw the dice and pick up the number of segments the dice shows and add them to your Sidney.

❹ Continue to play until *all* the segments have been chosen. At the end of the game, the exact number must be thrown to take the last segment.

❺ The player with the longest Segment Sidney is the winner.

SEGMENT SIDNEY PLAYING PIECES

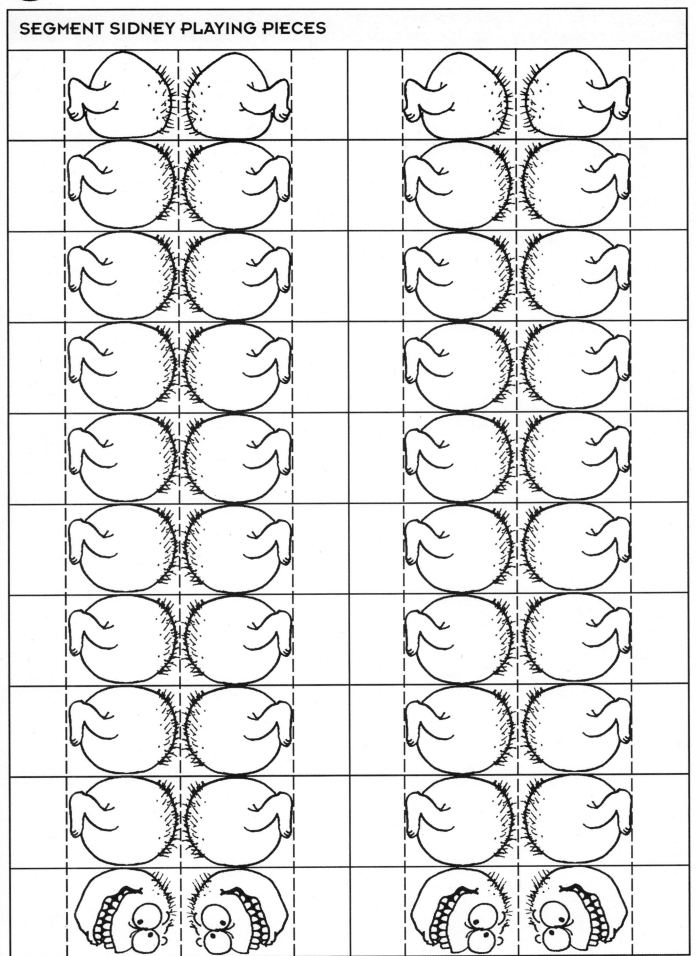

RECORD SHEET FOR SEGMENT SIDNEY (EXTENSION)

Name

_____

↔ [ ]

body
segments

My Segment Sidney has [ ] pairs of legs.

[ ] all segments X 2.5cm = [ ] cm.

He is [ ] cm long.

He is the [ ] longest.

Name

_____

↔ [ ]

body
segments

My Segment Sidney has [ ] pairs of legs.

[ ] all segments X 2.5cm = [ ] cm.

He is [ ] cm long.

He is the [ ] longest.

Name

_____

↔ [ ]

body
segments

My Segment Sidney has [ ] pairs of legs.

[ ] all segments X 2.5cm = [ ] cm.

He is [ ] cm long.

He is the [ ] longest.

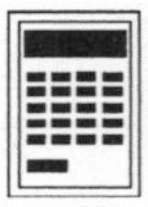

Name

_____

↔ [ ]

body
segments

My Segment Sidney has [ ] pairs of legs.

[ ] all segments X 2.5cm = [ ] cm.

He is [ ] cm long.

He is the [ ] longest.

MONDAY'S CHILD

TEACHING CONTENT

☆ Practising knowing the days of the week in sequence (SSM: 4a; T: A)

PREPARATION

Assembling the game: Copy the cards and weekly prism on to card. Cut out the cards. Staple or glue the prism into shape. It shows the relationship between the dice throws and the order of days. If you think the children already know this, do not use the prism. Make sure they know that they must put down Saturday before Sunday.

Introducing the game: Show the children the cards for this game, putting them down in order as you say the poem. Discuss the days of the week. Do the children know how many there are, or can they count them as you repeat the poem and then say the individual names? Write all the days of the week and their abbreviations on the board. Draw a box round each abbreviation as on the cards. Read out one of the poems given on page 58. Can the children remember what happens when I sneeze on Wednesday? What happened to Solomon Grundy on a Friday?

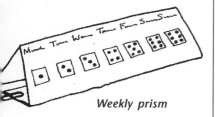

Weekly prism

HOW TO PLAY

This is a group game for any small number of players. Scatter the cards face up in the centre of play. Let the players sort out the playing order. Each player then throws the dice and picks a card. The cards are placed face up in an orderly row in front of the players. The cards can only be picked up and added to the row in the order of the week, that is 1 for Monday, 2 for Tuesday, and so on. A 6 is needed for Saturday and the game ends with another 6 for Sunday. The child putting Sunday in place is the winner. If the player throws a number other than the one needed for the next card, she does nothing and play passes to the next player.

TEACHER'S ROLE

Note that the rhyme has been reworded regarding Sunday. The traditional words are '…But the child that is born on the Sabbath day, Is bonny and blithe, and good and gay.' While the poetry is much better, the sentiment is not easy to understand in a modern multi- and non-faith society. The Sabbath is not necessarily Sunday, and even more awkward are the words 'blithe' and 'gay' which have changed their meanings somewhat. If you decide to replace the words on the card with the original ones, please explain their meanings in this context.

After the game, have a short question-and-answer session: For which day of the week does the child have far to go? What does 'Mon' mean? Roll the dice. Which day of the week is it?

GAME VARIATION

For a longer version of this game, stack a full set of cards for each player in the centre of play. Either sort the cards into seven stacks, one per day, or put them in one pile which the players have to sort through themselves. Challenge every player to make a complete week by throwing the dice in turn and picking up the cards in order. The first one to do so wins.

HOW TO PLAY MONDAY'S CHILD

For 2 or more players

YOU NEED: the Monday's child cards, a dice and shaker.

❶ Scatter the cards face up in the centre.

❷ Take turns to throw the dice and pick up the card that goes with that number BUT the cards can only be picked up in the order of the week: Monday, Tuesday, Wednesday, Thursday, Friday, Saturday, Sunday. Make a row with the cards.

❸ If you throw any number other than the one needed for the next card, do nothing and pass the dice to the next person.

So: if ⏐Mon⏐ ⏐Tues⏐ are already out, the next number must be 3 for Wednesday.

❹ The player who throws a 6 to put Sunday in place is the winner.

PHOTOCOPIABLE POEMS

Sneeze on Monday, sneeze for danger,
Sneeze on Tuesday, kiss a stranger,
Sneeze on Wednesday, get a letter,
Sneeze on Thursday, something better,
Sneeze on Friday, sneeze for sorrow,
Sneeze on Saturday, see your sweetheart tomorrow.

(Ask the children when is 'tomorrow' – Sunday.)

Solomon Grundy
Born on Monday
Christened on Tuesday
Married on Wednesday
Took ill on Thursday
Worse on Friday
Died on Saturday
Buried on Sunday
That was the end of Solomon Grundy.

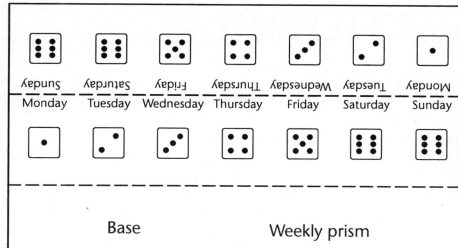

Base

Weekly prism

Glue this flap

Monday's child

is fair of face.

Tuesday's child

is full of grace.

Wednesday's child

is full of woe.

Thursday's child

has far to go.

Friday's child

is loving and giving.

Saturday's child

works hard for a living.

But the child born on Sunday

is happy and good all day.

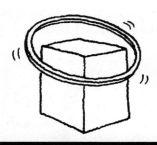

PHOTOCOPIABLE PAGES

Three-dimensional shapes sheets (Special Section) 141–144, construction sheet 140, 'How to play' sheet 62, record sheet 63.

FOR CONSTRUCTION

Thin and thick card, paper, scissors, adhesive, Plasticine or metal washers or marbles, ten large paper plates.

FOR PLAYING

Four 3-D shapes from Special Section, at least five 'hoops', 'How to play' sheet, record sheets, coloured crayons or pens.

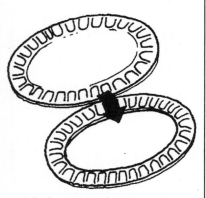

Stick the remainder of the plates together rim to rim.

3-D HOOPLA

TEACHING CONTENT

★ Recognising and naming four 3-D shapes (SSM: 2a; RS: A)
★ Identifying the properties of 3-D shapes (SSM: 2b; RS: B)
★ Making models of 3-D shapes (SSM: 2b; RS: B)

PREPARATION

Assembling the game: Copy the nets of the three-dimensional shapes from the Special Section (pages 141–144) on to thin card and assemble each one according to the instructions given on page 140. Stick the shapes on to a thick cardboard base to make the hoopla. There should be a generous space around each one to allow the 'hoop' to fall over it easily. The disadvantage of sticking down the shapes is that the players cannot examine the face of the shape that is stuck to the baseboard. If you would prefer the shapes to be free-standing, they will need some extra weight inside them as crumpled paper alone will not provide a heavy enough base. A lump of Plasticine would be best, or, alternatively, metal washers or marbles. However, make sure that whatever is used lines the base of the shape. Instead of fixing the positions of the shapes, draw the outline of each one on to the baseboard. Each shape can be returned to its outline if it is dislodged and before any player casts a hoop, the positions of the shapes can be checked and adjusted if necessary. Also, having the shapes separate allows the game to be packed away easily after use and the shapes to be returned to general class use. Make at least five hoops. Cut a circular hole in the middle of each of ten paper plates. The holes should be large enough to fit easily over any of the three-dimensional shapes. Stick the plates together in pairs face to face. The resulting hoops are quite substantial and easy to hold.

Introducing the game: Look at the three-dimensional shapes together. Ask the children to guess, and then count, how many faces the shapes have. This can be noted on the top record sheet (photocopiable page 63).

HOW TO PLAY

This is a simple game for two or more players, focusing on counting the number of faces on each three-dimensional shape. The throws are recorded on the record sheet on page 63.

Give each player a different coloured pen or crayon to mark their throws on the record sheet. Let them have five throws each. Tell them that the idea is to get as many faces as possible. Every hoop that settles over a shape is recorded in the player's own colour as a ring over that shape at the top of the record sheet. Throws that miss are not recorded. When the throws have been drawn on to the sheet, the next player has her turn. The game can end after one round with everyone counting up how many faces they have scored. The winner is the one with the most. Play more rounds if you wish.

'3-D hoopla' is an ideal solo game for a child with a few moments to spare. It can be played in a corner with the player recording his throws on a record sheet or just telling you how well or badly he is doing.

TEACHER'S ROLE

The record sheet is not essential to the game. You may prefer the players just to show you where their throws landed after each round. This would give you the opportunity to ask each player which shapes she got the hoops over and which she missed. Repeated addition of the same number is also reinforced through this game as multiples of the same shape are ringed and their faces need to be totalled.

GAME VARIATION

Set a goal of ringing a set number of faces. This will force the players to think about the number of faces they have collected already and the best shapes to get the ones they require. This can be made even more difficult by saying that they have to throw the exact number of faces.

EXTENSION

☆ Recognising faces, edges and corners of 3-D shapes (SSM: 2a; RS: B)

This is a more advanced version of '3-D hoopla' and takes the players through the various properties of the three-dimensional shapes. For this game, the throws are recorded on the lower part of the record sheet on page 63. Have three rounds of throws. In the first round count only faces; in the second round count only edges; and in the third round count only corners. Every face, edge and corner is worth one point. Total the points and work out the finishing positions. Allow the children to use calculators to help them with the adding, if necessary.

From this game, you will be able to evaluate how well the children understand the various properties of three-dimensional shapes as they identify them. Emphasise the correct words for these properties and gently encourage the children to use the words 'cube', 'cuboid' and 'prism'. How far you want to go with 'triangular' will depend on the children.

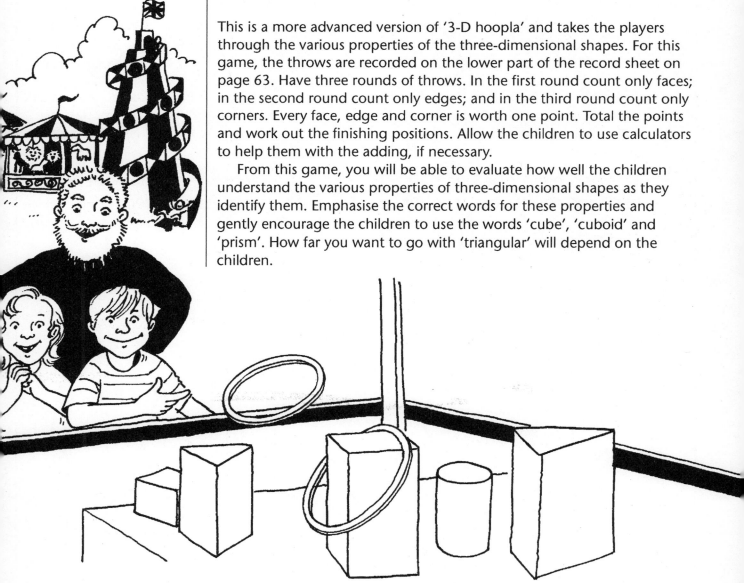

HOW TO PLAY 3-D HOOPLA

For 2 or more players

YOU NEED: the hoopla, hoops, a different-coloured crayon for each person, a record sheet.

❶ Take turns to throw the hoops at the hoopla.

❷ A hoop must fall over a shape to count.
Hoops which miss or only half cover a shape do not count, but the player cannot have more throws.

❸ Ring your throws on the record sheet.

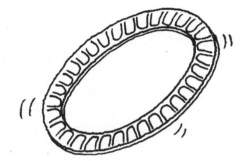 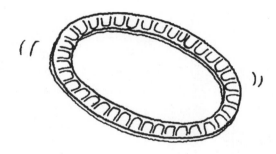

❹ When everyone has had a turn and the record sheet has been filled in, count the number of faces each player has scored.

❺ The player scoring the most faces wins.

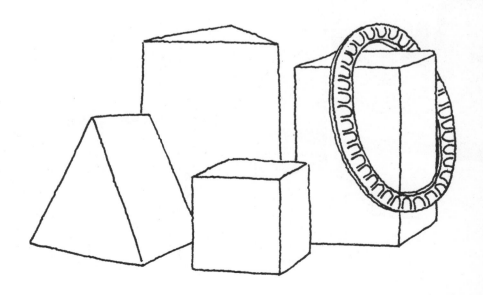

RECORD SHEET FOR 3-D HOOPLA

Ring your throws.

cube	cuboid

☐ faces	☐ faces

small triangular prism	long triangular prism
☐ faces	☐ faces

Name	☺ faces 1st round	✎ edges 2nd round	✗ corners 3rd round	Totals	Final positions

SHAPES DOMINOES

TEACHING CONTENT

☆ Matching shape to shape (SSM: 2c; RS: A)
☆ Examining the properties of shapes (SSM: 2a; RS: A/B)

PREPARATION

The dominoes sheet (page 66) is best copied directly on to card and then cut up. The record sheet is an optional extra.

HOW TO PLAY

Shuffle the dominoes and place the pack face down. Tell each player to take four dominoes and keep them in their hands, hidden from the other players. The first player should put down a domino and pick up a replacement. Play passes on to the next player who has to put down a domino with a shape that matches one of the two at either end of the domino line. Double dominoes are placed across the domino line.

WHAT YOU NEED

PHOTOCOPIABLE PAGES
Shapes dominoes sheet 66, 'How to play' sheet 65, record sheet 67 (optional).
FOR CONSTRUCTION
Card (optional), scissors.
FOR PLAYING
Shapes dominoes, 'How to play' sheet, record sheet (optional), a different-coloured crayon for each player (if using record sheet).

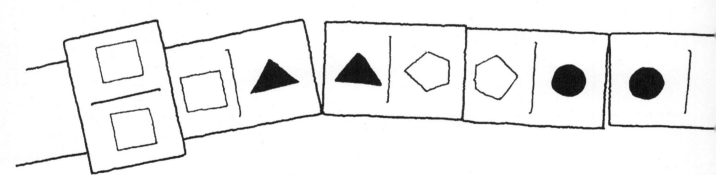

For every domino put down, a new one should be picked up. If a player cannot match the shapes available, he still has to pick a domino from the pack which can be used the next time round. If the record sheet is to be used to record the game, give each player a different coloured crayon with which to colour in on the sheet each domino he puts down. Play continues until a player gets rid of all his dominoes to win. If no one gets rid of all their dominoes, the player with the least dominoes left is the winner.

TEACHER'S ROLE

Once the children understand the rules of the game, there should be little need for you to intrude. After the game, reinforce the ideas involved by putting down particular dominoes and asking: Which shapes match here? What are the names of these shapes? How many sides (or angles) has the shape on this end got? Can you put the dominoes in order of number of sides (or angles)? Which shape has the most? Which shape has the least? Which dominoes have circles on them? Which have squares? Similar questions could be drawn out from the completed record sheet.

Using a copy of the record sheet, ask the children to identify angles and right angles, and write inside each shape its number of sides or angles.

HOW TO PLAY SHAPES DOMINOES

For 2 to 4 players

YOU NEED: the shapes dominoes.

❶ Shuffle the dominoes and place the pack face down.

❷ Take four dominoes each and keep them hidden from the other players.

❸ The first player puts down a domino and picks up the top card from the pile as a replacement.

❹ The next player has to match one of the shapes on his or her dominoes with one of the shapes at either end of the domino line. Continue like this.

❺ Whenever a domino is put down, a new one must be picked up. If you cannot match any dominoes, you must still pick up another domino. All new dominoes can only be played from the next round.

❻ Continue to play until one of you has no more dominoes and wins, OR, with all the dominoes picked up, no one can put one down. Then the player with the least dominoes wins.

RECORD SHEET FOR SHAPES DOMINOES

Name

red

Name

blue

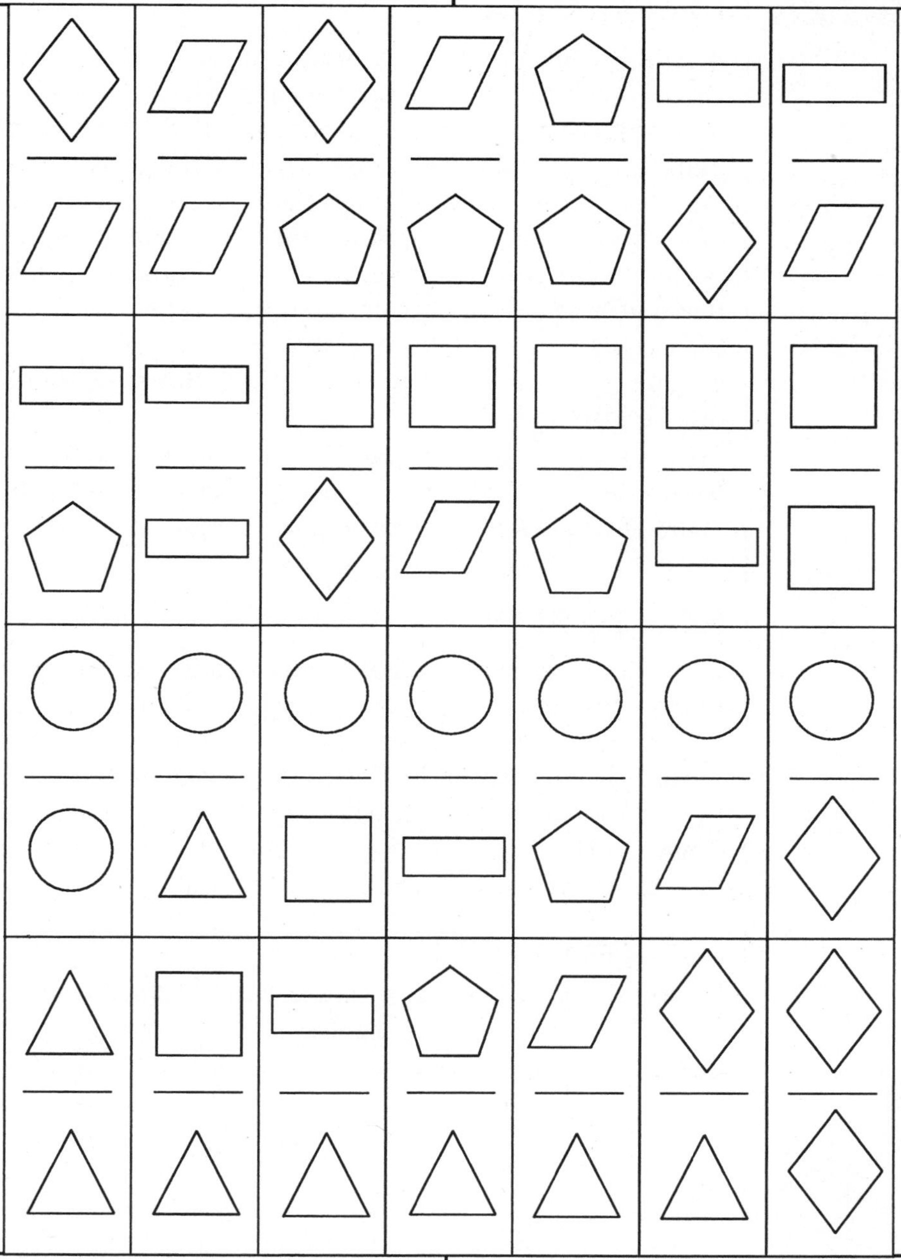

Name

green

Name

yellow

TREASURE CHEST

TEACHING CONTENT

☆ Practising common positions, for example 'in' or 'below', in relation to one object (SSM: 3a; PM: A)
☆ Relating physical positions to a diagram (SSM: 3a; PM: A)
☆ Using common words to describe position (SSM: 3a; PM: A)

PREPARATION

Assembling the game: Copy or mount the treasure chest (page 70), the crown (page 69) and the position and 'Knave of Hearts' cards (page 71) on to card. Assemble the treasure chest and crown, holding the flaps with paper clips until the adhesive is dry. The chest and crown would be improved if they were coloured before being assembled. The cards should be uncoloured except, perhaps, for the 'Knave of Hearts' card. If the position cards are coloured, the chest will appear solid and the concept of being able to see that the crown is not inside it will be more difficult for the children. For a pack make at least three sets of the position cards but include only one 'Knave of Hearts' card. However, there can be more than one 'in' card in the pack.

Introducing the game: Explain that the aim of the game is for the children to put the king's crown away safely before the Knave of Hearts steals it away. Discuss where the safest place might be and introduce the idea of the treasure chest.

HOW TO PLAY

Check that the treasure chest is closed and that the crown is in the centre of play. Shuffle the cards and place them face down in the middle too. Each player takes the top card and puts the crown where the card directs. The used cards are left in a discard pile face up to one side. They will not be used again. The player who puts the crown in the chest wins. If the 'Knave of Hearts' card is drawn everyone loses and the game ends as he has stolen the crown away.

TEACHER'S ROLE

During the game, observe how well the children assimilate the information on the word/diagram cards. Throughout the game point out what the drawings represent. Ask the players to read the words, or guess them by taking clues from the drawings. After the game, use the cards with the crown and a classroom table to show that the drawings can be applied to another similar object. Extend this by drawing a stylised chair on large sheets of paper or by making a set of similar cards showing a chair, and playing the game using a real chair. In this way the children will see that the same words can describe a variety of objects and will begin to understand the relationship between the diagrams on the cards and the real-life situation.

HOW TO PLAY TREASURE CHEST

For 2 or more players

YOU NEED: the treasure chest, the crown, the position cards including a 'Knave of Hearts' card.

❶ Before playing, check that the lid of the treasure chest is closed.

❷ Shuffle the position cards. Place the pack face down in the centre of the table along with the treasure chest and the crown.

❸ One by one, turn over the top card and put the crown where the card shows. Leave the used card on a discard pile face-up.

❹ The player who puts the crown IN the chest is the winner.

❺ If the 'Knave of Hearts' card is shown, the game ends. Everyone has lost! The knave has stolen away the crown.

CROWN

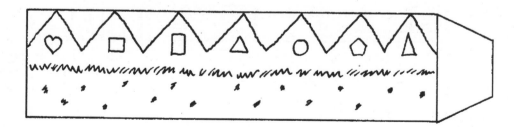

Cut out crown.
Curve crown round and glue or tape flap.
Hold securely in place with a paper clip until
the adhesive is dry.

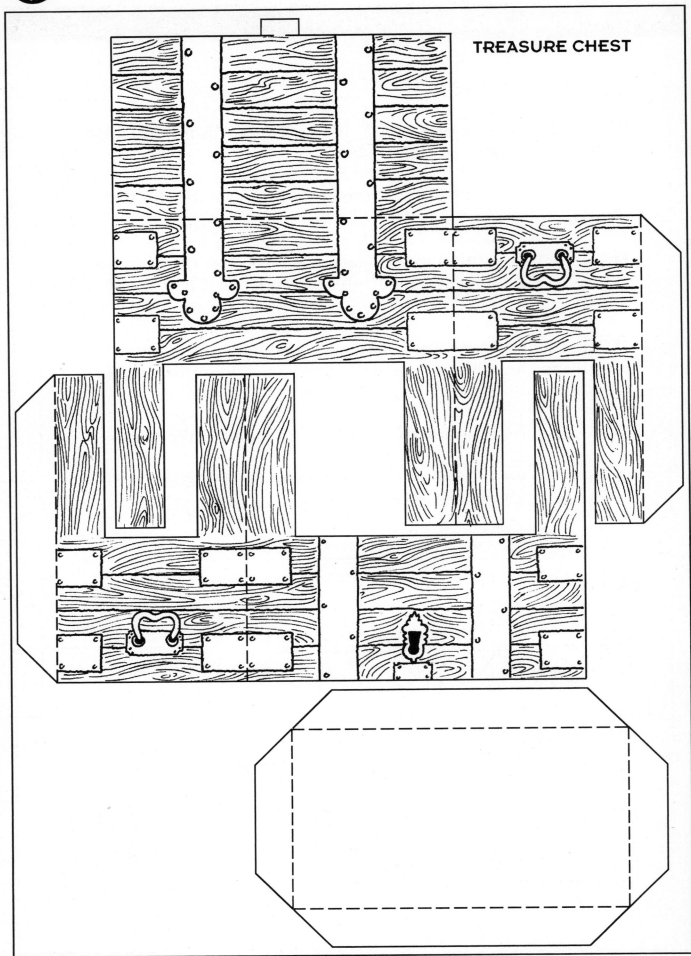

TREASURE CHEST

X3

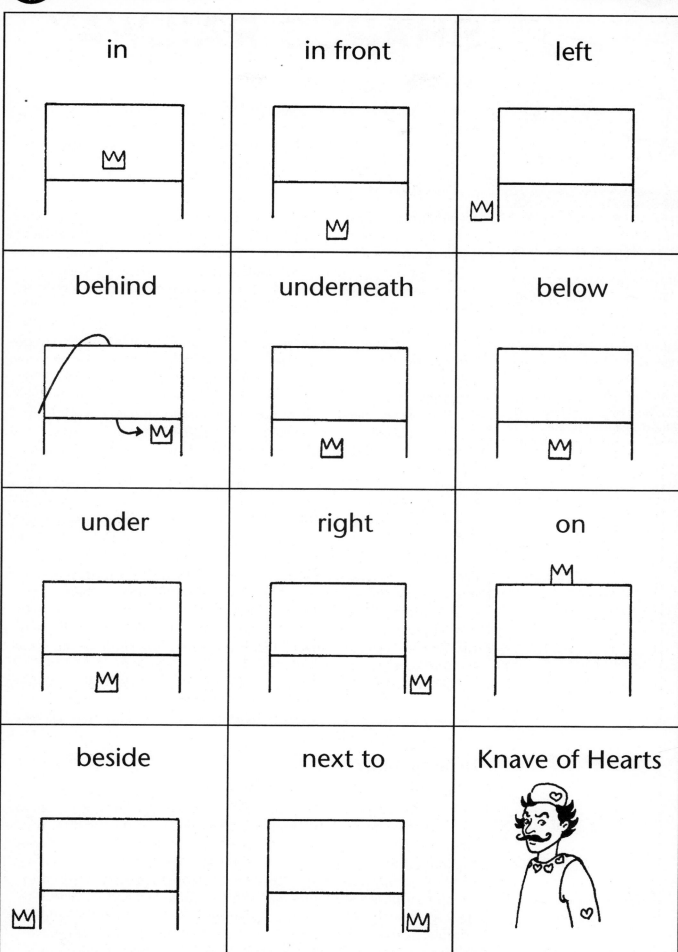

in	in front	left
behind	underneath	below
under	right	on
beside	next to	Knave of Hearts

SHAPES RAILWAY

WHAT YOU NEED

PHOTOCOPIABLE PAGES
Track game board sheet 75, centre piece and playing pieces sheet 76, 'How to play' sheet 74, record sheet 77, 2-D shape cards (Special Section) pages 138–139.

FOR CONSTRUCTION
Card, scissors, adhesive, paper clips, coloured crayons or pens.

FOR PLAYING
Railway game board, train playing pieces, a set of at least 24 2-D shape cards, a dice and shaker, record sheet (optional).

TEACHING CONTENT

☆ Recognising 2-D shapes (SSM: 2b; RS: A)
☆ Identifying sides and angles of 2-D shapes (SSM: 2c; RS: A/B)
☆ Widening the scope of 2-D shapes beyond the basic circle, square, rectangle and triangle (SSM: 2b; RS: B)

PREPARATION

Assembling the game: Copy the track game board on page 75 four times and arrange the pieces on a baseboard, with each piece at right angles to the next. Make sure the rails line up. The space in the middle can either be filled with the photocopiable centre piece with the word 'Cards' printed on it or just left empty. Colour each corner position in a different colour to match the trains playing pieces. Leave the small square at the corner of each straight track and the track itself uncoloured. Colour the centre 'Cards' spot and the various 'cards' spaces on the track in orange. The four train playing pieces are best copied directly on to card and then coloured, but if they are to be mounted, colour them beforehand. Then stick them into shape, securing them with paper clips until the adhesive is dry. You will also need some of the two-dimensional shapes cards from the Special Section (photocopiable pages 138–139). Which ones you choose to use will depend on how much experience the children have had of the shapes. There should be at least 24 cards in the pack. If you use the 'circle to hexagon' set (photocopiable page 138), this will require a minimum of four copies of the sheet. Before the game you will need to decide on an appropriate objective – you might decide that the winner will be: the player who gets the most shape cards, or, the player whose shapes have the most angles (or the most sides), or, the player whose cards have the most right angles, or, the player with the most shapes with four sides. All these are perfectly valid as the cards show all these characteristics. You will need to fill in your chosen objective and how to win on the 'How to play' sheet before giving it to the children. There is also an optional record sheet which can be cut into strips for each player.

Introducing the game: Introduce this game by talking to the children about trains: Who has been on a train? Are trains today like those used in this game? What kinds of trains are those in the game? What do you call people who travel on trains? Where is the nearest station? Then explain the chosen object of the game.

HOW TO PLAY

Shuffle the cards and place the pack face down in the centre of the board. The players choose a train each and put it on the 'Start' space in the same coloured corner. Then they take turns to throw the dice. To start a player must throw a 6 or 5. (This is an optional rule.) For each square, the front of the train is lined up with the far edge of the square that it is officially occupying. If a train stops on a 'Card' space, that player takes the top card from the centre pile *without looking at it* and transfers it to her own corner coloured corner space *still face down*. Each train must go completely round the track until it comes back to its own finish space. (Throwing an exact number to finish could be another optional rule.)

When all the trains are back in their corners, the players can turn over their cards and count the particular properties that you decided upon as the object of the game, for example sides or angles. If all the cards are claimed before every train is back at its own corner, end the game there and tell everyone to look at their cards immediately.

TEACHER'S ROLE

The railway layout enables the players to acquire cards, which are then used for a specific purpose. In this game, this has a maths objective, but they could be language cards, place-names, or the names of children in the class as passengers. The possibilities are almost endless.

The cards are left face down until the end of the game to increase the suspense, and to give you the opportunity to be present when the cards are checked. Help those children who are unsure of the sides and/or angles and so on to count them. Go over the numbers by asking each child how many sides or angles are on her cards. Include a short question-and-answer session about the shapes: their names, their numbers of sides, their numbers of angles, and which shapes have right angles. Ask which shapes they do not know the names of and encourage them to try saying them anyway.

The record sheet allows the children to identify the angles and sides of the shapes they have got. This is not as complicated as it might seem. However, each possible objective would be recorded in a different way. If the objective is to have the most shapes or only particular shapes, the children should colour in all or the appropriate shapes they collected. If the objective is to have the most angles, the children should mark all the angles they collected with curves, or squares if the objective is to collect right angles. If the objective is to have the most sides, the children should mark each side they have collected with a dash on the shapes on the record sheet.

GAME VARIATIONS

The track game board is open to adaptation. Instructions can be written directly on to the board into double spaces, enlarged by having a line deleted, or you can make two sets of railway cards – one penalty set and one bonus set – which could be kept in two of the four empty spaces on the board to the right of 'FINISH'. The instructions could govern the speeds of the trains: accelerating the trains (moving them on so many squares) by means of green signals, level-crossing open and so on; or slowing them down (making them go back so many squares or miss turns) by means of level-crossing closed or track repairs. Alternatively, the instructions might add or subtract shapes or specific characteristics. The bonus and penalty cards, linked to colour-coded squares on the board, could similarly add or deduct angles, sides or shapes. This would fit into a game where each train goes round the board until a set number of cards have been collected.

HOW TO PLAY SHAPES RAILWAY

For 2 to 4 players

YOU NEED: the track game board, the trains playing pieces, a set of 2-D shape cards, a dice and a shaker.

❶ Choose a train each and put it in the same coloured corner on the 'START' space.

❷ Shuffle the cards and place them face down in the centre of the board.

❸ Throw a 5 or 6 to start. Then take turns to move round the board according to the numbers you throw.

❹ If your train lands on 'card', pick up the top card WITHOUT looking and put it FACE DOWN in your train's corner.

❺ Each train must go right round the board and back to 'FINISH'.

❻ To finish you must throw an exact number.

❼ When ALL the trains are back in their corners, turn over the cards and count. The winner is the one with the most

_____.

x4

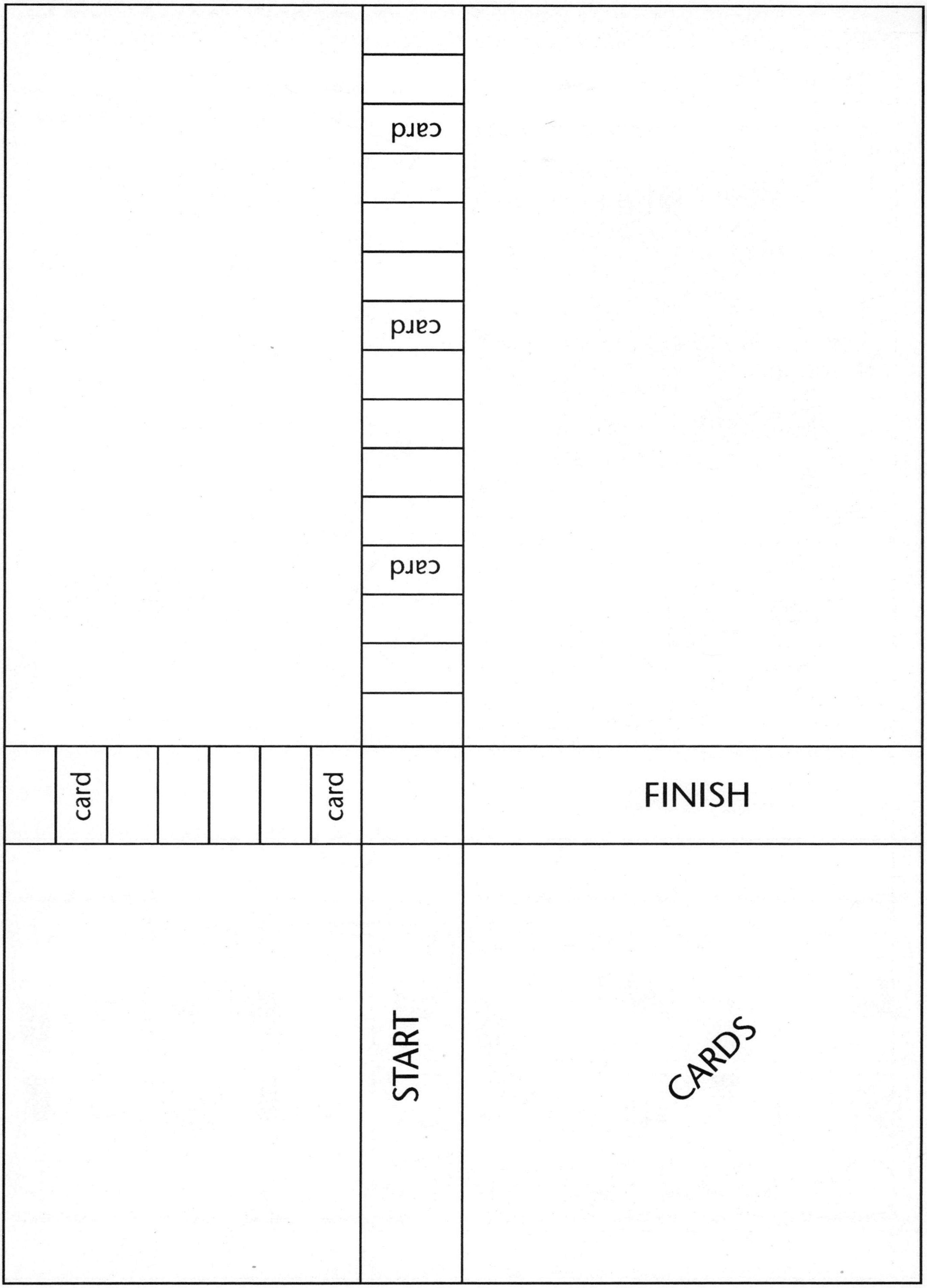

card

card

card

card

card

FINISH

START

CARDS

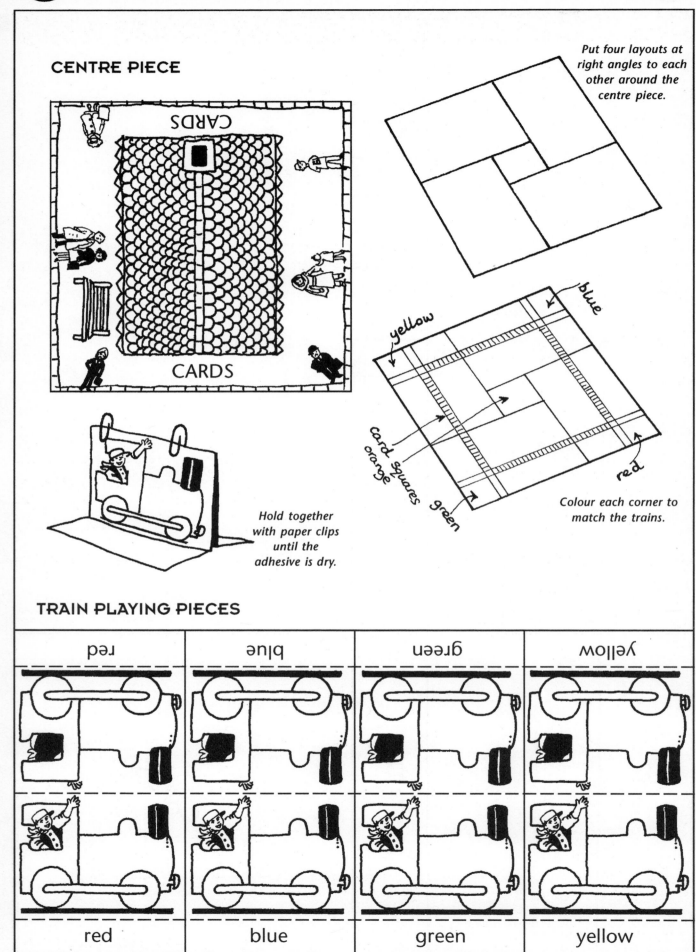

CENTRE PIECE

CARDS

CARDS

Put four layouts at right angles to each other around the centre piece.

Hold together with paper clips until the adhesive is dry.

yellow

blue

Card squares
orange

green

red

Colour each corner to match the trains.

TRAIN PLAYING PIECES

red	blue	green	yellow
red	blue	green	yellow

PHOTOCOPIABLE GAMES

SHAPES RAILWAY

RECORD SHEET FOR SHAPES RAILWAY

Name

  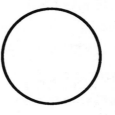 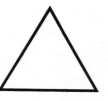 

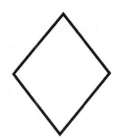  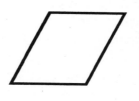 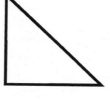 

 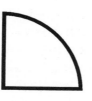  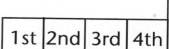

Draw in the sides or angles you got.

1st	2nd	3rd	4th

Name

 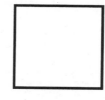 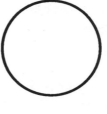 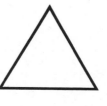 

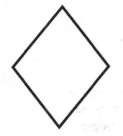   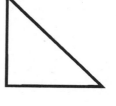 

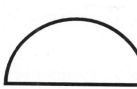 

Draw in the sides or angles you got.

1st	2nd	3rd	4th

VEGGIES

TEACHING CONTENT

☆ Covering a space with non-standard units (SSM: 4a; ME: A)
☆ Using squares as a unit of measurement (SSM: 4a; ME: A)

PREPARATION

Assembling the game: Make four copies of the garden plot (photocopiable page 80) and one of the 'How to play' and centre piece sheet (photocopiable page 79). Cut off the centre piece. This acts as a 'planting guide' for the players to follow. Mount the four garden plots at right angles to each other around the centre piece on a thick card baseboard. (See diagram on page 79.) Copies of the record sheet on page 81 are used to make the vegetable cards playing pieces.

Make four sets of vegetable cards by copying photocopiable page 81 directly on to card four times. Cut up the sheets into individual cards. The game is enhanced if all the items are coloured as 'naturally' as possible. As each player has a particular plot and no movement or interchange of pieces is involved other than covering the plot, there is no need to colour each playing area in a distinct colour. An ordinary dice and shaker are needed also. The record sheet is optional. If you wish to use it, further paper copies of page 81 will be required for the players to follow.

Introducing the game: Talk about growing vegetables like the ones in the game. Who grows them in their gardens? Whose dad or mum or grandparents have an allotment? What is an allotment? Use the planting guide to bring in the idea of 'area' by talking about how each plant has to have a space (area) around it to get enough water, sunlight and air and so plants such as vegetables are usually planted in rows not too close together. In this game the players are gardeners. Who is going to plant the biggest 'area'?

HOW TO PLAY

Put all the vegetable cards in the centre. In turn, each player throws the dice and picks out the same number of cards as the number thrown. The rows of 'veggies' have to be planted in complete rows in the same arrangement as shown on the planting guide. The first player to plant all eight rows wins. Stop the game there and work out the other game positions from the number of vegetables each player has 'planted'.

TEACHER'S ROLE

After the game, talk about how many rows each player completed, how many vegetables they 'grew' of each type and, lastly, how big an area they covered, as shown by the number of cards they put down. Each using a record sheet and planting guide, the children can colour in the veggies they have 'planted' to match their plots.

HOW TO PLAY VEGGIES

For 2 to 4 players

YOU NEED: Veggies game board, a set of vegetable cards for each player, a dice and shaker.

❶ Choose a vegetable plot each and sort out the playing order.

❷ In turn, throw the dice and take that number of vegetable cards.

❸ 'Plant' your plot as shown on the planting guide.

❹ The first 'gardener' to complete all eight rows is the winner.

❺ Stop here and count up how many vegetables you have each 'planted'. Who came second? Third? And fourth?

CENTRE PIECE
Planting guide

cauliflowers · onions · courgettes · celery · beans · lettuce · beetroot · tomatoes

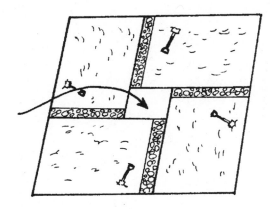

Arrange the four garden plots at right angles around the centre piece.

x4

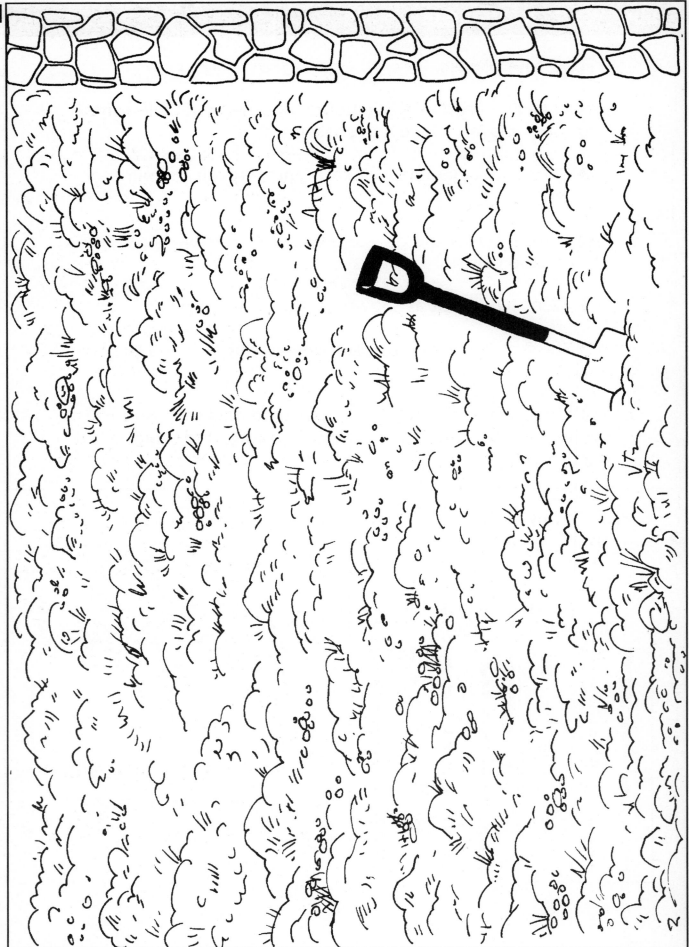

CARDS/RECORD SHEET FOR VEGGIES

Name _____

x8

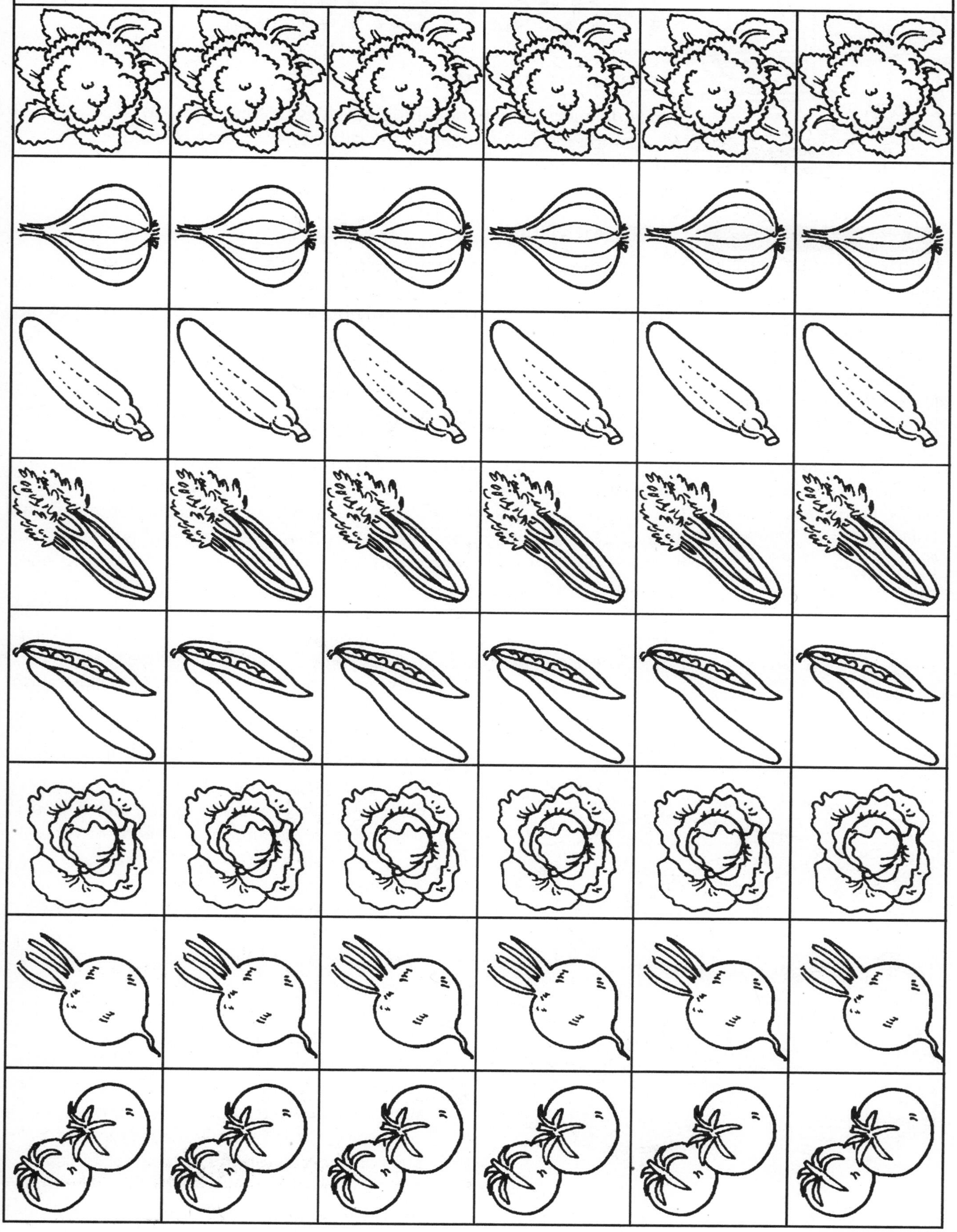

HOLDALLS/ TRUCKERS

TEACHING CONTENT

☆ Simulating real-life measuring activities (SSM: 1c; ME: A)
☆ Comparing and estimating the capacity or volume of various containers (SSM: 4a; ME: A)
☆ Using a comparative measuring container (SSM: 4b; ME: A)

PREPARATION

Make a measuring container from a clear-sided plastic container larger than any of the containers to be measured. Stick a blank strip of paper on the side. If you want to keep the strip as a record, attach it with sticky tape at its top and bottom. The group record sheet is an optional extra. Assemble the rest of the game so that it can be played with liquid (as 'Holdalls') or with sand (as 'Truckers').

Holdalls: To play the game with liquid, you will need six different-shaped containers of a fairly similar size: large plastic squash bottles, fancy-shaped shampoo bottles, mugs, plastic sweet boxes, toy buckets, toy kitchen pots and pans and so on. Do not use containers where their capacity can be compared just by sight. Also do not use glass containers or containers that have held toxic chemicals, even if they have been thoroughly cleaned out. Attach a dice number, written on to paper with a waterproof marker pen, to each container with sticky tape.

Truckers: To play the game with sand, you could use the above containers or you could use six different-dimensioned boxes, again of a fairly similar size. These can be made into trucks with windows and wheels, and dice numbers, drawn or pasted on. (See illustration opposite.)

The characteristics of each container cannot be changed for future games. To off-set this, the containers are identified by dice numbers on labels which can be swapped about. The symbolic representations on the record sheet make it a little more difficult to 'pass on' information about the relative sizes of the containers to other children after the game.

HOW TO PLAY

In turns each of the six players selects a container (or truck) by throwing the dice. If that number container has already been claimed, he should have another throw. Each container (or truck) is filled with liquid (or sand) which is then poured through a funnel into the measuring container. A line is drawn on the strip on the measuring container to indicate the quantity and marked with the dice number. The measuring container is then emptied.

When all six have been chosen and measured, the final positions can be seen on the label of the measure with the biggest first and smallest last. The winner may be the one with the biggest, or smallest, container. Fill in the record sheet together to indicate which container was the biggest, which was second and so on.

TEACHER'S ROLE

Capacity tends to be the 'poor cousin' of measurement teaching, especially when it involves water. All too often it is seen as messy. Yet all that are needed are sensible precautions, such as the use of a funnel to direct the liquid or sand and to work over a bath or large sink.

The capacities of similar-sized or different-shaped containers cannot be assessed easily by sight alone; they have to be compared physically. In this game all the containers are compared in one measure, common to them all, and their capacities recorded on a scale as the game progresses. This is more simple than relying purely on comparative measurement of one container against another, when a systematic procedure for finding which is heaviest may be employed (see 'Fat cats' pages 102–107).

There is no easy word for measuring capacity like 'weighs'. You will need to use the word 'holds' plus 'more', 'the same' or 'less' and 'biggest' and 'smallest' which can be used equally for mass or weight. Bring in 'capacity' for liquids and 'volume' for sand, though the two are interchangeable to some extent.

EXTENSION

✫ Simulating real-life measuring activities (SSM: 1c; ME: B)
✫ Estimating and measuring the metric capacity or volume of various containers (SSM: 4a; ME: B)
✫ Using a metric measuring container (SSM: 4b; ME: B)
✫ Acquainting the children with the vocabulary of volume and capacity and the metric units and their abbreviations 'litre', and 'l', also ½l, ¼l, and 'millilitres' and 'ml' (SSM: 4a; ME: C)

Metricising the 'Holdalls/Truckers' game is very easy. Instead of the measuring container, use standard measuring jugs and scoops. Alter the record sheet so that it shows litres, millilitres or cubic centimetres, in accordance with the size of the containers. If you are measuring in litres, quite large boxes could be used as trucks – large enough for cuddly toys to be the truckers. Throughout, draw the players attention to the correct form of abbreviation. At the end of the game, you might like to ask the group to add up the respective volumes using a calculator in order to practise the manipulation of standard units and their subdivisions.

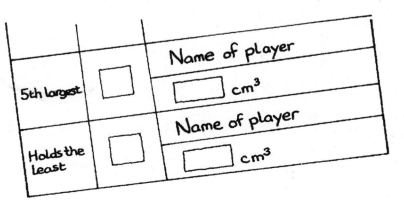

HOW TO PLAY HOLDALLS/TRUCKERS

For 6 players

YOU NEED: six containers (or six trucks), a funnel, a measuring container, a jug, water (or sand), a dice and shaker.

❶ Shake the dice and take the container (or truck) with the same number.

❷ If it has been claimed already, throw until you get the number of an unclaimed container (or truck).

❸ Fill your container with water (or your truck with sand) and then pour this carefully into the measure.

❹ Mark the level of the water (or sand) on the paper strip with a line and the dice number.

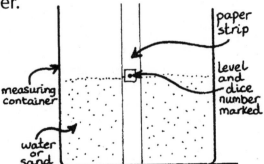

❺ Empty the measure.

❻ When all six containers (or trucks) have been measured, work out the final game positions. The top mark is the biggest; the one at the bottom is the smallest.

GROUP RECORD SHEET FOR HOLDALLS/TRUCKERS

Holds the most		Name of player
2nd largest		Name of player
3rd largest		Name of player
4th largest		Name of player
5th largest		Name of player
Holds the least		Name of player

WHAT YOU NEED

PHOTOCOPIABLE PAGES
*'Dummy' cards sheet 89,
Dummy game board sheet 88,
'How to play' sheet 87.*
FOR CONSTRUCTION
Card, scissors, adhesive.
FOR PLAYING
*Four three-dimensional shapes
(Special Section pages 141–
144), game board, hoop,
'Dummy' cards.*

DUMMY

TEACHING CONTENT

★ Identifying 3-D shapes by their faces, edges and corners
(SSM: 2c; RS: B)
★ Knowing the number of features of 3-D shapes (SSM: 2c; RS: B)

PREPARATION

If necessary, make the four three-dimensional shapes from the Special Section (photocopiable pages 141–144) according to the instructions given on page 137 and place them in a hoop or a circle of paper. Copy the 'Dummy' cards (page 89) and the game board (page 88) on to card. The game board does not necessarily have to be mounted on to card; a photocopy should be good enough.

HOW TO PLAY

Shuffle the cards and place the pack face down between the hoop and the game board. One by one, each player should take the top card and turn it over. If it shows a number, the player can claim a shape if she can say what connection there is between the number and the shape. To claim a shape, it is not enough to just say 'It is the cube' or something similar. The claim must explain itself. So if a 6 is shown, the claim could be 'It is a cube because it has six faces.' If a claim is upheld by the group, the player can take the shape from the hoop and put it into its place on the game board. The used card should be put on a new pile face up. If a claim is not upheld or if the number cannot be applied to an unclaimed shape, play goes on to the next player. If a 'Dummy' card is shown, the player drawing it must miss a turn. The player putting the last shape in place on the game board is the winner.

TEACHER'S ROLE

This is a self-regulating group game, so you can observe from a distance to see how well the players cope with the claims and counter-claims. Your intervention and adjudication should be a last resort.

After the game, play a flash card game with the cards, hold up a card and ask the players to identify the possible shape. Also lay out the cards and ask the players to pick out all the cards to do with a particular shape, for example 6, 12 and 8 for a cube.

Below are the geometrical features of the four shapes:			
Cube	6 faces	12 edges	8 corners
Cuboid	6 faces	12 edges	8 corners
Small tri prism	5 faces	9 edges	6 corners
Long tri prism	5 faces	9 edges	6 corners

GAME VARIATION

The game can be extended by using commercially-available three-dimensional shapes. These would not have the features highlighted, but the children should be able to apply their experience to 'blank' shapes. Additional cards with appropriate numbers and a larger game board including the new shapes would be needed.

HOW TO PLAY DUMMY

For 2 or more players

YOU NEED: a hoop, the four three-dimensional shapes, the Dummy cards and the game board.

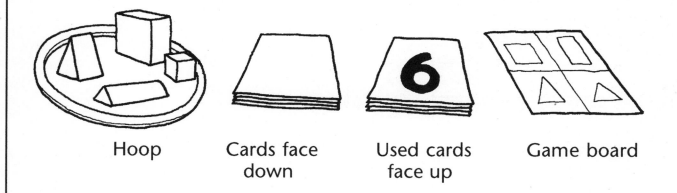

Hoop   Cards face   Used cards   Game board
              down   face up

❶ Put the shapes in the hoop.

❷ Shuffle the cards and then put them in a pack face down.

❸ In turn, show the top card.

❹ If you want to claim a shape, you must say what the connection is between the number on the card and the shape. If everyone agrees, you can move the shape from the hoop to the game board.

❺ If the number only matches a shape already on the game board, play goes on to the next player.

❻ If you draw a dummy, miss a turn.

❼ The player who puts the last shape on to the game board wins.

GAME BOARD

GAME BOARD

5	5	6	6
6	6	8	8
9	9	12	12

WHAT CAN IT BE?

TEACHING CONTENT

☆ Recognising different types of movement (SSM: 3a; PM: A)
☆ Practising straight (translation) and turning (rotation) movements (SSM: 3a; PM: B)
☆ Using right angles as a measurement of turn (SSM: 3b; PM: B)

PREPARATION

This is a paper-and-pencil game in which the children follow instructions to make a picture on a grid. It is a solo puzzle, though the children can compare their results. Indeed, it can be played by the whole class at one and the same time. Make enough copies of the instruction sheet (photocopiable page 91), that when they are cut into the three lettered strips, there are sufficient to distribute one to each player: so some will get A, some B and some C. The instructions are given in both diagrammatic and written form. If you think that the children need either the diagrams or the written aspect of the game emphasising then delete the other column. Each player also needs a drawing sheet (photocopiable page 92) on which to carry out the instructions on the strip.

HOW TO PLAY

Each player begins at the starting point on the drawing sheet and draws a thick line on to the grid according to the instructions on their strip, working from top to bottom.

TEACHER'S ROLE

Ensure that the players have had practice in right and left. During the game, draw out from the children the fact that instructions to turn left, right, up and down are variations of rights angles. When the drawing is finished right angles can be identified and counted.

Let the children go on to make their own drawings on further copies of the drawing sheet or on squared paper and then work out instructions for them. They can then hide the original drawings and ask friends to re-draw the pictures using only their instructions. Finally compare the two drawings.

WHAT YOU NEED

PHOTOCOPIABLE PAGES
Drawing sheet 92, instruction strips sheet 91.
FOR CONSTRUCTION
No special requirements.
FOR PLAYING
Pencils or coloured pens.

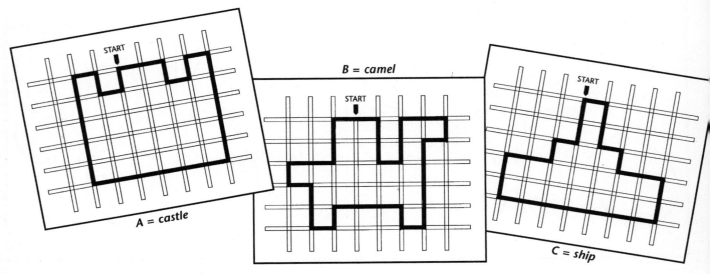

A = castle

B = camel

C = ship

INSTRUCTION STRIPS

A
Follow these instructions to draw a shape on your grid.

right 2

down 1

right 1

up 1

right 1

down 5

left 6

up 5

right 1

down 1

right 1

up 1

B
Follow these instructions to draw a shape on your grid.

right 1

down 2

right 1

up 2

right 2

down 1

left 1

down 4

left 1

up 1

left 3

down 1

left 1

up 2

left 1

up 1

right 2

up 2

right 1

C
Follow these instructions to draw a shape on your grid.

right 1

down 2

right 1

down 1

right 2

down 2

left 7

up 2

right 2

up 1

right 1

up 2

WHAT CAN IT BE? DRAWING SHEET

You can go in four directions: left, up, right, down.
Colour in the track as you go.

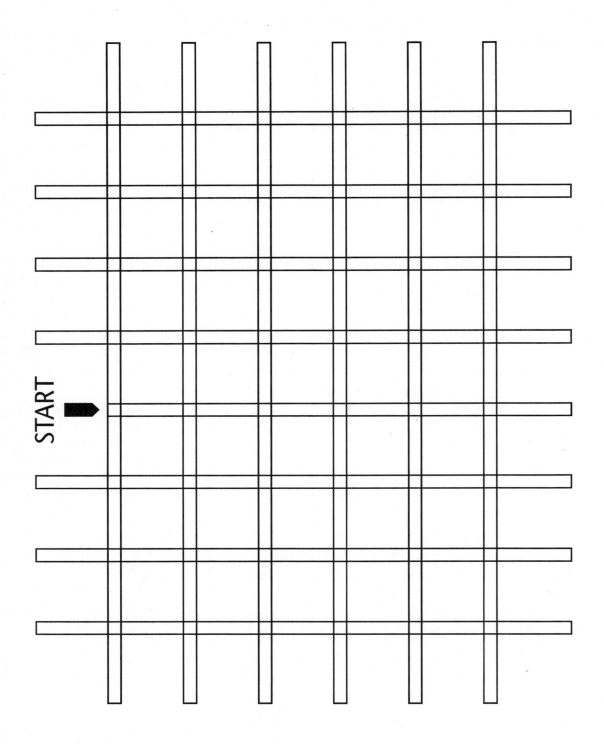

START ➤

Drawn by _____

BRITISH ISLES

TEACHING CONTENT

☆ Experiencing clockwise and anticlockwise turns (SSM: 3b; PM: B)

☆ Understanding angle as a measure of turn (SSM: 3b; PM: B)

PREPARATION

Assembling the game: There are two versions of this game using the same baseboard (photocopiable page 96), but with a mask added to investigate clockwise and anticlockwise (photocopiable page 97) or a pointer added to investigate angles of turn (also given on page 96).

For the clockwise/anticlockwise game: Copy or mount the baseboard and mask on to card. Colour them when the adhesive is dry. Cut out and fasten the mask to the base using a paper fastener or a card rivet. Fix the paper fastener in place with sticky tape across the back. Doing this will also protect the children's fingers. You will need to photocopy a record sheet for each player also.

For the angles game: Copy or mount and colour in only the baseboard and the pointer. Cut out and attach the pointer in the centre of the base with a paper fastener. Again you will need a record sheet for each player.

Introducing the game: Before the game, go through the various pictures shown on the wheel. The children may be unaware of the traditions of national flags and emblems. Ask them in which country we live. Go into detail about each country and discuss their patron saints. The association of flags and patron saints with particular countries goes back to the Middle Ages. The armies 'adopted' the saints and offered prayers to them in times of battle. For example, Richard I adopted St George (patron of England) as the protector of the Crusaders. The flags of Sts Andrew, George and Patrick were combined into the Union Jack. The contentious issue of Irish politics has been avoided by using the saltire of St Patrick, which was added to the Union flag in 1801. The Red Dragon of Wales is an ancient symbol, probably introduced by the Romans, and attributed to Uther Pendragon and King Arthur, and Cadwallon, King of Gwynedd (5th century), among others. Can the children find out about the origins of the English rose, the Scottish thistle and so on?

WHAT YOU NEED

PHOTOCOPIABLE PAGES

British Isles baseboard and pointer sheet 96, mask sheet 97, record sheet 98, 'How to play' sheet 95.

FOR CONSTRUCTION

Card, scissors, adhesive, coloured pens or crayons, paper fasteners or card rivets.

FOR PLAYING

British Isles wheel with mask or pointer, a dice and shaker, 'How to play' sheet, a record sheet for each player.

HOW TO PLAY

Clockwise/anticlockwise game: Line up the mask to show the flag of St George. The players then take turns to throw the dice. If the number thrown is odd, the player moves the mask clockwise for that number of divisions. If the number is even, the mask is moved anticlockwise. Each player colours in on her record sheet the corresponding item at which the mask stops. The first player to colour in a full set of emblem, flag and famous place for one country is the winner.

Angles of turn game: This version uses the baseboard with the pointer. Starting anywhere, the pointer is turned through the same number of angles as the dice throw shows and all in the same direction (clockwise). Otherwise it is the same game.

TEACHER'S ROLE

During the clockwise/anticlockwise game, check that the players understand the difference between the two directions. If they are having difficulty, further work on the concept may be necessary. Show the children analogue clock-faces, discuss how the traffic goes round a roundabout and ask them to use their arms to physically show a clockwise sweep from left to right and an anticlockwise sweep from right to left.

During the angles game, check that the children understand the correlation between the numbers on the dice and the number of angles turned. Afterwards, strengthen the children's perception of the angles by linking them to right angles. Aim for them to see that any three consecutive angles on the board make a right angle. Give the children paper photocopies of the baseboard (page 96) on which to colour in the 12 right angles possible, shading a different set of four on each copy. If the children have touched on the 3 times table, draw up a table of angles together: 3 angles = 1 right angle, 6 angles = 2 right angles, 9 angles = 3 right angles and so on.

GAME VARIATION

For a degrees version of the angles game, write '30°' between each short line on the baseboard. Make a degrees dice by sticking labels on a play brick – 30°, 60°, through to 180°. The children can then move the pointer through the appropriate number of 30° divisions. Afterwards, make a list of 30° divisions up to 360° and ask the children to identify them using the baseboard and ring the right angle numbers on the list – 90°, 180°, 270° and 360°.

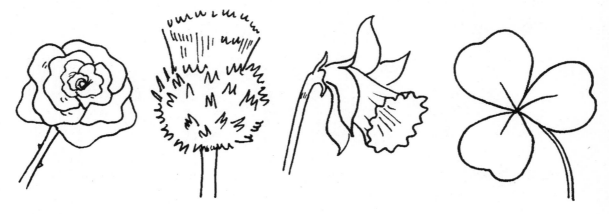

HOW TO PLAY BRITISH ISLES

For 2 to 4 players

YOU NEED: the British Isles wheel, a pen or pencil in a different colour, a record sheet for each player, and a dice and shaker.

CLOCKWISE/ANTICLOCKWISE GAME:

❶ Put the opening of the mask on the flag of St George:

❷ Take turns to throw the dice.

❸ Move the wheel round the same number of spaces as the number on the dice. The dice number also shows the direction.

Move clockwise for odd numbers:

      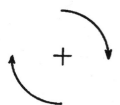

Move anticlockwise for even numbers:

      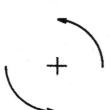

❹ Colour in each picture on your record sheet that the wheel stops at.

❺ The first player to get a full set – flag, emblem, and famous place – wins.

ANGLES OF TURN GAME:

❶ Put the pointer on any line pointing to a symbol to start.

❷ Take turns to throw the dice and move clockwise that number of angles.

❸ As before, colour in each symbol you stop at on your record sheet. The first player to colour in a full set wins.

BASEBOARD

POINTER

MASK

RECORD SHEET FOR BRITISH ISLES

Forth Bridge

Customs House

Caernarfon Castle

Nelson's Column

Colour in each picture you land on.

RIGHT ANGLE OR ¼ TURN

TEACHING CONTENT

☆ Recognising right angles (SSM: 3b; A: B and PM: B)
☆ Moving through one, two, three or four right angles (SSM: 3b; PM: B)
☆ Moving through ¼, ½, ¾ and 1 whole turns (SSM: 3b; PM: B)

PREPARATION

Assembling the game: This paper-and-pencil game requires the four players to make moves on the game board (page 101) according to the throw of one of two special dice and to be the first to colour in one circle on each of the four lines. Each player needs a different coloured pen or pencil. Copy and assemble the two special dice (nets given on photocopiable page 100), one of which shows right-angled turns and the other shows quarter to whole turns. Alternatively, the faces can be stuck on a plastic cube or play brick. Choose which of the dice to use. It is a good idea for the children to play both versions of the game so they can equate right-angled turns with quarter turns. The game can be made more permanent by mounting page 101 on to card and laminating it. Then coloured counters are used to cover the circles instead of colouring them in.

Introducing the game: Before the game, make sure that the children understand right angles and fractions of a turn. Ask the players to match the faces of the two types of dice. The children could play with them, rolling them to see if they can get a matching pair.

HOW TO PLAY

This is a game for two to four players. Each player in turn throws the chosen dice. The dice will show a turn which the player works out every time from the central arrow position, colouring in a circle on the line he reaches. There can be only one colour per line, so if the player has already coloured in a circle on that line, play passes on to the next player. The first player to colour in a circle on all four lines wins.

WHAT YOU NEED

PHOTOCOPIABLE PAGES
'How to play' and dice sheet 100, game board sheet 101.

FOR CONSTRUCTION
Scissors, adhesive, a plastic cube (optional).

FOR PLAYING
A '¼ turns' dice, a 'right angles' dice, a different coloured pen or a set of four counters for each player, a game board.

TEACHER'S ROLE

After the game, extend the children's understanding of turn by moving a toy figure through the turns according to the players' dice throws. Develop the concept by making the turns from the last circle stopped at. Using a three-dimensional figure gives the children something to associate with so that they can imagine making the turns themselves.

GAME VARIATION

Allow more than one circle of the same colour on a line and let the game progress until all the circles are coloured. The final positions are worked out according to the number of circles each player has coloured. The one with the most is the winner.

HOW TO PLAY RIGHT ANGLE OR ¼ TURN

For 2 to 4 players

YOU NEED: the game board, a coloured pen for each player, a 'turns' dice and shaker.

❶ Sort out the playing order.

❷ Take turns to throw the dice. The dice shows a turn that you must work out from the central arrow.

❸ Colour in a circle on the line you get to in your colour. If you have already coloured in a circle on that line, play passes on to the next player.

❹ The first player to colour in one circle on each of the four lines is the winner.

DICE NETS

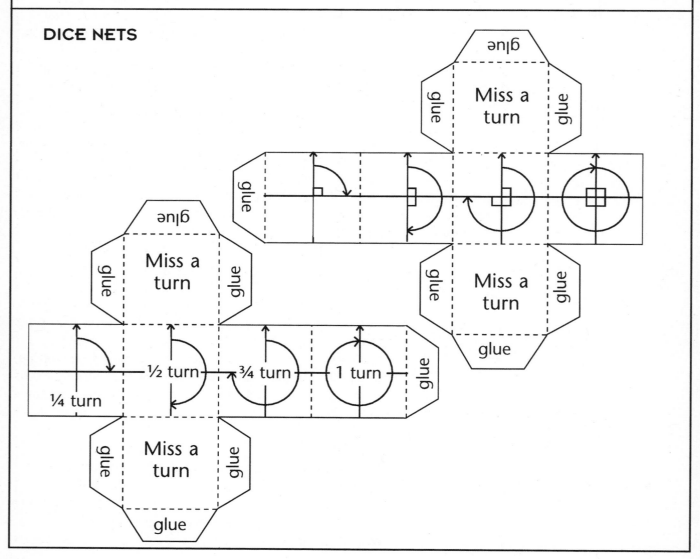

RIGHT ANGLE OR ¼ TURN GAME BOARD

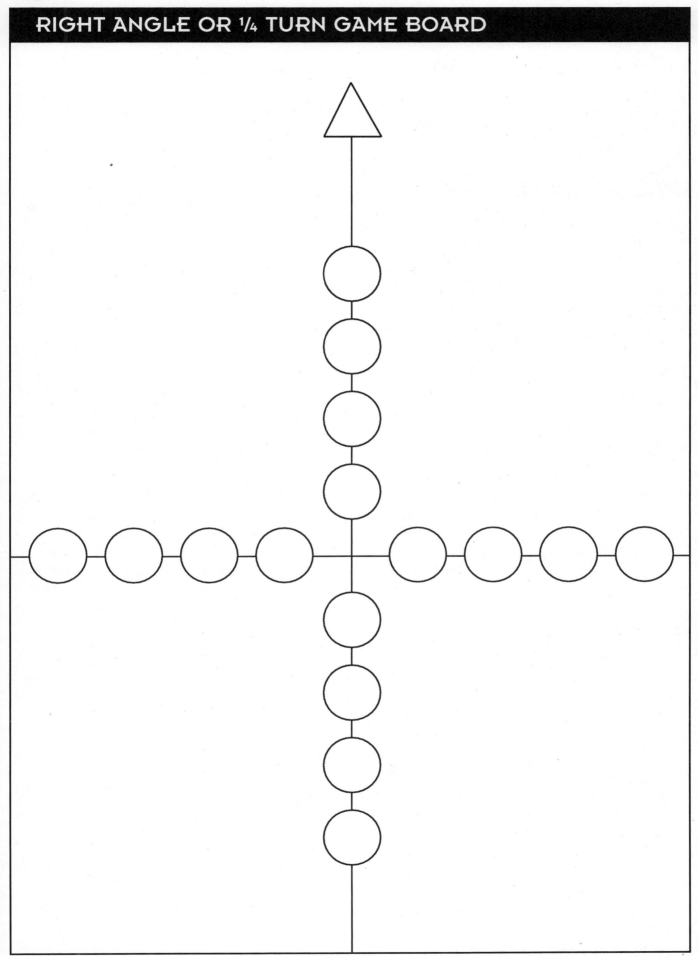

PHOTOCOPIABLE PAGES
Fat cat and box net sheet 105, 'How to play' sheet 104, record sheet 106.

FOR CONSTRUCTION
Card, adhesive, scissors, coloured pens or crayons, six small bags, some marbles or other small, dense weights.

FOR PLAYING
Six fat cats of different weights, a dice and shaker, a simple balance, record sheet, 'How to play' sheet.

1. Assemble the boxes and attach one to each cat. 2. Put a different small weight in each box. 3. Seal the box to stop counting/cheating.

FAT CATS

TEACHING CONTENT

☆ Practising weighing (SSM: 1c; ME: A)
☆ Comparing and estimating weights (SSM: 4a; ME: A)
☆ Using scales in a functional manner (SSM: 4b; ME: C)
☆ Using the vocabulary of weighing in a purposeful way (SSM: 4a; ME: A)

PREPARATION

Copy, or mount, six cats and box nets (photocopiable page 105) on to card. The cats can be coloured, but as their main means of identification stick a dice number on to each cat. Assemble the boxes and stick one on to the back of each cat. Away from the children, put a small bag of marbles in each box. Seal the lid lightly with sticky tape so that the weight cannot be estimated by counting. Vary the number of marbles in each bag: one in one bag, three in another, five in another and so on. Experiment until each cat is definitely different in weight/mass to the others. Alternatively, use dissimilar weights such as steel washers, pebbles or nails. The weights should in no way correlate to the dice numbers. The players will need to use the record sheet in order to get the maximum value from the game.

HOW TO PLAY

This is a game for six players. Each player throws the dice and picks up the same numbered cat. If that cat has already been chosen, the player throws again. When everyone has a cat, the problem is to find which is the heaviest. This requires a process of elimination. You will need to be on hand to take the group through the early stages of this process. Tell the children to weigh cat 1 against cat 2 on the balance. The heavier cat will sink down and the lighter cat should be taken off and replaced with cat 3. Again, the heavier cat will sink and cat 4 should take the place of the lighter cat. Do the same with cat 5 and cat 6. At the end of this process, the cat that remains on the lower side of the scales is the heaviest cat of all. Tell the children to use the same process to find the second heaviest, the third heaviest and so on until all the cats have been put in order. As each cat's position is identified write the corresponding dice number and the name of the player who chose that cat on to the record sheet. The winner is the player with the heaviest cat.

TEACHER'S ROLE

This game appears much more complicated than it really is. It is much easier to compare the weight/mass (or capacity) of a group of objects using standard metric measures, which have numerical values, than using non-standard measures. This game introduces the children to an algorithmic method for comparing a group of six objects; that is, a systematic procedure for finding which is heaviest. This methodical system of elimination simplifies what is otherwise a very difficult exercise in experimentation and observation. The principle behind the game can be applied to volume as well as weight/mass. You may need to explain the symbols used on the 'How to play' sheet for level scales and a heavier

scale and introduce the simple vocabulary of 'heavier' and 'heaviest'. 'Mass' is the correct term for 'weight' in this context. Introduce it as soon as you feel it is appropriate.

This is not a game where you can stand back and let the children work it out among themselves. When the players have chosen their cats, stress the difficulty of estimating the comparative weights. They can try weighing with their hands; but is one cat really heavier than the other? Now show them how they can weigh one cat against another easily with the scales. However, putting them into order is still not so easy, so introduce the system of elimination. The game can be reversed, with 'lightest' as the winning objective. The winning order on the record sheet is from the bottom up.

EXTENSION

★ Practising weighing (SSM: 1c; ME: B/C)
★ Comparing metric weights (SSM: 4a; ME: B/C)
★ Estimating weights in grams (SSM: 4a; ME: C/D)
★ Using scales in a functional manner (SSM: 4b; ME: C)
★ Using the vocabulary of weighing and the abbreviation 'g' in a purposeful way (SSM: 4a; ME: B)

For this game it is assumed that the class are familiar with weighing in grams, that they know what 'grams' are, and what 'g' represents. Before the game, set up the weights for the fat cats and the corresponding record sheet (photocopiable page 107). Here the game has been devised for weights between 100g and 500g and 'over 500g'. If you are using these parameters, then the weights should be approximately in the middle of each zone, for example, 250g for 200–300g. If a weight is too near the border of the zone, it may cause confusion as to which zone it belongs in. You will need one weight for each zone, so that all the spaces will be filled in on the record sheet at the end of the game. (Of course, you can use alternative weight ratios. For example, the target weights could be multiples of 250g, or even in multiples of 1kg. The cats and the boxes would have to be made bigger and stronger to do this.)

Introduce the game by explaining that all six fat cats are in the final of the 'Feline Slimmer of the Year Competition'. Their owners have kept their podgy pets on fat-free diets of skimmed milk, lean steak, trimmed bacon, and reduced-fat cheese. However, one of the furry friends has been cheating and slipping out at night to steal other pets' food and to gobble up the local wild birds and mice. As each cat 'steps up' to the competition scales, which one do the children think is going to be at the target weight, and win, and which cat will be in 'the cheating zone'?

As before each player throws the dice to select a cat. Each cat is then weighed in grams and its dice number is entered in to the appropriate weight zone square on the record sheet. This will automatically determine the final game positions. As the game progresses, observe how the children cope with standard weight. At the end, get the group to write down the exact weights of the cats, making sure that they use the correct abbreviation. Ask them to add the weights together using a calculator. Do all the cats together weigh more than 1kg, or 2kg? As they probably cannot put all the cats on a balance scale to check their calculation, they may have to use a different type of scale. What type do the children suggest?

HOW TO PLAY FAT CATS

For 6 players

YOU NEED: six fat cats, a dice and shaker, a simple balance and record sheet.

❶ Throw the dice to pick a cat. If the cat with that number has already been chosen, throw again.

❷ NOW use the balance to find the heaviest cat by weighing one against another.

Start like this:

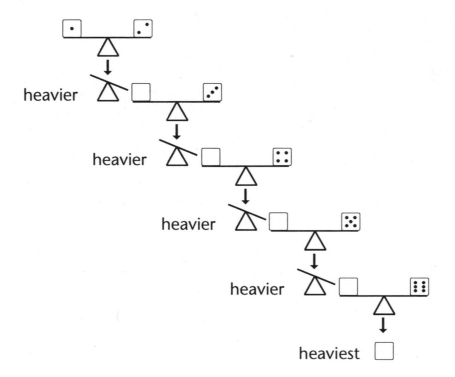

❸ Fill in the heaviest cat's number on the record sheet.

❹ Now take out the heaviest cat, and do the same weighing to find the second heaviest. Start with ⚀ (if it was not the heaviest... if it was, start with ⚁ and miss ⚀ out).

❺ Now do the same for the other positions on the record sheet. The winner is the one with the heaviest cat.

FAT CAT AND BOX NET

x6

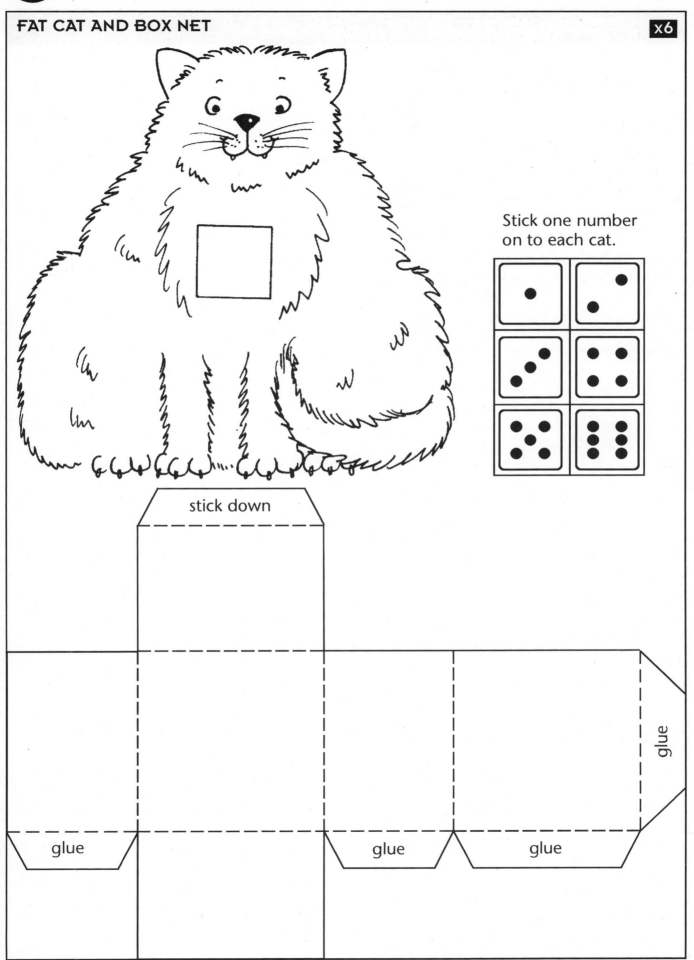

Stick one number on to each cat.

stick down

glue

glue

glue

glue

GROUP RECORD SHEET FOR FAT CATS

Heaviest		Name of player
2nd heaviest		Name of player
3rd heaviest		Name of player
4th heaviest		Name of player
5th heaviest		Name of player
Lightest		Name of player

RECORD SHEET FOR FAT CATS (EXTENSION)

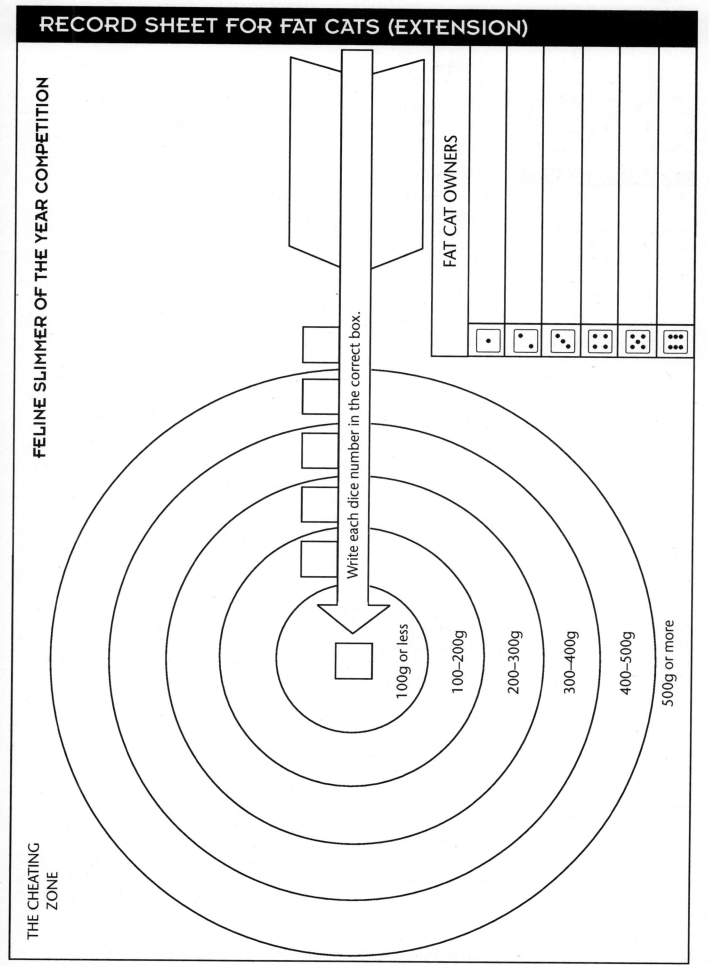

FELINE SLIMMER OF THE YEAR COMPETITION

Write each dice number in the correct box.

FAT CAT OWNERS

100g or less

100–200g

200–300g

300–400g

400–500g

500g or more

THE CHEATING ZONE

WHAT YOU NEED

PHOTOCOPIABLE PAGES
Biker game board sheet 110, centre and playing pieces sheet 111, 'How to play' sheet 109.

FOR CONSTRUCTION
Thick and thin card, scissors, adhesive, coloured pens or crayons, paper clips.

FOR PLAYING
Biker game board, a translations and rotations' dice and shaker, a biker playing piece of each player, 'How to play' sheet.

BIKER

TEACHING CONTENT

☆ Following direction signs to move along a route (SSM: 3a; PM: B)
☆ Familiarising the children with translations and rotations (SSM: 3a; PM: B)

PREPARATION

Assembling the game: Mount four copies of the game board sheet (photocopiable page 110) on to a thick card baseboard. The sheets should be arranged at right angles to each other with the centre piece – the market square – in the space in the middle. The finished board comprises of four self-contained routes, not one big one. To help reinforce this, colour the circles on each sheet differently; so there is a red route, a blue route, a green route and a yellow route.

The four biker playing pieces should be copied or stuck on to card and coloured in the same colours as the routes and then folded and glued individually. Assemble the 'translations and rotations' dice or stick the faces on to a plastic cube or brick. Hold the bikers and dice with paper clips until all the adhesive has dried.

Introducing the game: The game board and playing pieces represent a bicycle road race, such as the *Tour de France*, which the children may have seen on television. Do any of the children ride a bicycle? Do they know what hand signals should be used for turning right or left when on a bicycle? Talk about road safety and let some of the children pretend to be the traffic on a chalked-out roadway while others give the directions to turn left or right or move forwards. A collection of maze games culled from comics and magazines could be a stimulus for more investigation of routes, as could the Ancient Greek folk-tale 'Theseus and the Minotaur'.

HOW TO PLAY

Each player puts a biker playing piece on his chosen 'Start' circle. Each of the four players then takes turns to roll the 'movements' dice. They must throw a right-turn arrow to start. Each 'biker' can only progress to the third circle by throwing a left-turn arrow. Thus play continues to each subsequent circle. If there is any doubt, the player can hold the face of the dice over the next circle to check whether the directions match. The first biker to get into the market square wins. Play continues until second, third and fourth places have been determined.

TEACHER'S ROLE

Throughout the game, help the children when necessary. Get them to rotate the face of the dice around so that the various twists and turns of the arrows can be clearly seen. To emphasise the turns, pair the turns dice with a normal 1–6 dice and give the children squared paper and a pen with which to record their throws. Tell them to draw each turn on to the squared paper and then draw a straight line, in that direction, for the number of squares shown on the number dice. So a right-turn throw and a 5, would mean drawing a right turn followed by a line five squares long. This could be a record of the biker game or played separately, the winner being the one who makes the longest continuous line.

HOW TO PLAY BIKER

For 2 to 4 players

YOU NEED: the game board, a biker for each player, a 'movements' dice and shaker.

❶ Each player must throw a right-turn arrow to start. Then take turns.

❷ Once on the second circle, you can only move your biker on to the third circle by throwing an arrow in its direction – a left-turn.

❸ To get to the fourth circle, a left-hand arrow has to be thrown and so on.

❹ The arrows on the circles must be obeyed. If your throw does not match the next arrow, play goes on to the next player.

❺ The first biker to get to the market place in the middle wins.

❻ Go on playing for second, third and fourth places.

x4

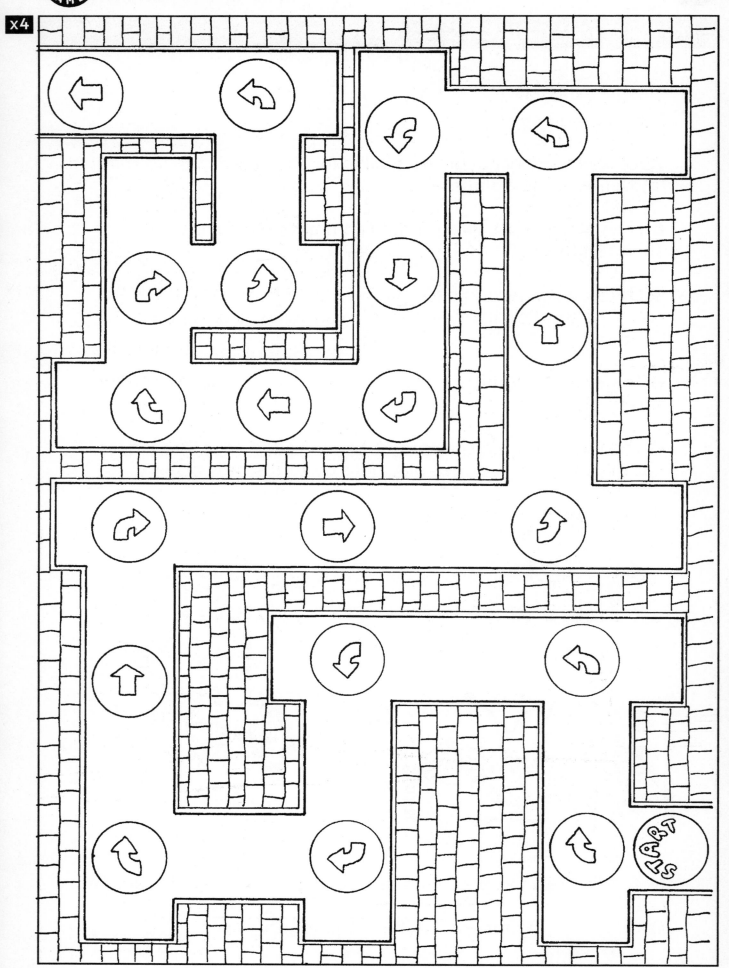

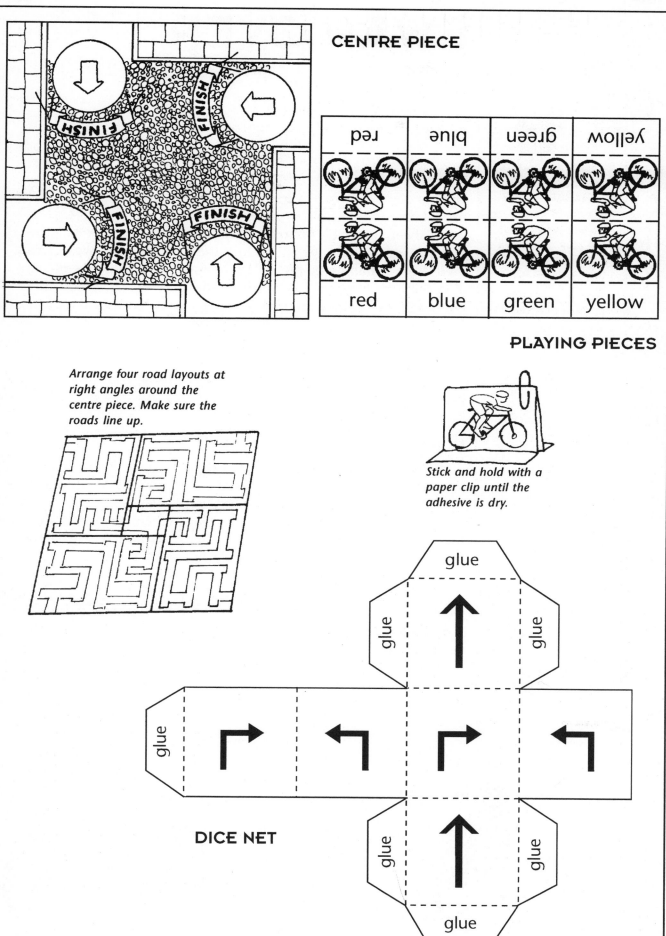

CENTRE PIECE

red	blue	green	yellow
red	blue	green	yellow

PLAYING PIECES

Arrange four road layouts at right angles around the centre piece. Make sure the roads line up.

Stick and hold with a paper clip until the adhesive is dry.

DICE NET

SWAP OVER

TEACHING CONTENT

☆ Practising the four points of the compass (PM: B)
☆ Recognising quarter turns/right angles (SSM: 3b; PM: B)

PREPARATION

This is a game for two players and uses a modified version of the 'Biker' game board (photocopiable page 110). Make one copy of the game board sheet, preferably on to card. Delete the arrows, but retain the circles. Write 'Start' in the last circle of the road system as well, so that there are two starting places. Colour one start in red and the other in blue. Stick the compass rose (given on the 'How to play' sheet) at the bottom of the board, with north pointing clearly to the top of the board (same direction as original finish arrow). Also make and colour in two biker playing pieces – one red and one blue. Assemble the spinner showing the four compass directions (also given on the 'How to play' sheet). Copy it on to card and cut it out. Then push a small sharp pencil or similar through the spinner as the pivot and fix it in place with dabs of PVA adhesive above and below the card.

HOW TO PLAY

In this game the players start at the opposite ends of the board and have to swap places. They can only go in the direction shown on the spinner. The 'How to play' sheet shows the first four moves made by each player. The rest have to be worked out by the players themselves. At some stage, there may be two bikers on one circle. This is permissible. The winner is the first player to swap to the other player's 'Start' circle.

TEACHER'S ROLE

During the game, ask the players which direction they need next, encouraging them to visualise their ideal spins. After the game, pick circles at random and ask the players what directions are needed to get to them from the two adjacent circles.

HOW TO PLAY SWAP OVER

For 2 players only

YOU NEED: one red and one blue biker, a game sheet and the compass spinner.

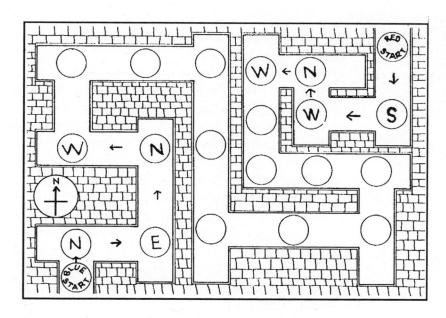

❶ Take turns with the spinner.

❷ You can only move if the spinner lands on the next direction you need. Otherwise play passes to the other player.

❸ The first four directions you need are shown above. You will have to work out the rest for yourselves.

❹ The first player to get to the opposite START is the winner.

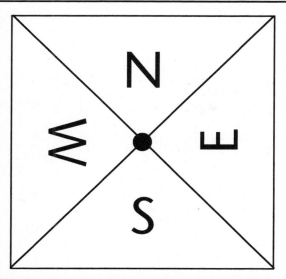

SPINNER

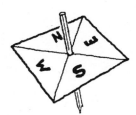

COMPASS ROSE

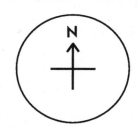

DICE TOWERS

TEACHING CONTENT

★ Measuring heights by comparison (SSM: 4a; ME: A)

★ Estimating heights (SSM: 4a; ME: A/B)

PREPARATION

Assembling the game: The tower blocks sheet (photocopiable page 117) is best copied directly, or mounted, on to card and then cut into strips. Fold each strip into three. The end flap goes behind the first side and is stuck in place. Hold it with a paper clip until the adhesive is dry. Make sure the overlaps are exactly level so that each block is touching the 'ground' all the way round. Finally cut the slits as indicated, so that the blocks can be fixed together. The blocks do not have to be coloured. A minimum of two sets of blocks are required for three players. The pieces are best kept in a box rather than being squashed in a bag.

Introducing the game: 'Dice towers' addresses the rather difficult aspect of length measurement – height. Height takes length measurement into the third dimension. Start by looking at flat heights, such as children standing against a wall. These are easier to compare initially than three-dimensional towers rising up from the ground.

Discuss the design elements of the towers. Why are they made from triangular blocks? One reason is that they are easy to make in this shape, but difficult to deform. Compare them with square blocks made in the same way and show how easily the squares deform. Another reason is that the sides can be perched at angles to each other and still remain stable. If squares are used, they are very difficult to put one on top of the other unless they were given a 'floor' and 'roof', so to speak.

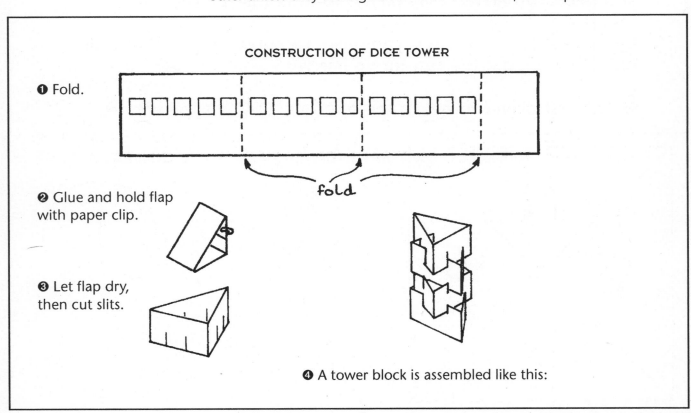

CONSTRUCTION OF DICE TOWER

❶ Fold.

fold

❷ Glue and hold flap with paper clip.

❸ Let flap dry, then cut slits.

❹ A tower block is assembled like this:

HOW TO PLAY

Place the tower blocks in the centre of play. Each player throws the dice and picks a block with the same dice number. If there is no block left with that number, play passes on to the next player. Each player builds a tower with her blocks as the game goes on. When all the blocks have been used, the game ends. The towers are compared and the highest wins.

TEACHER'S ROLE

You should not have to be involved much during the game as it is very simple, except perhaps to help the players with building their towers. During the game, encourage the children to estimate how their towers are progressing. Ask questions such as: Is yours the biggest tower? Do you think you are winning? Are you going to win?

The heights of the children's towers can be recorded using further copies of photocopiable sheet 117 cut into individual sections. Each building block strip would give three sections. These can be stuck on to vertical strips of paper and mounted in a high-rise cityscape display (see illustration).

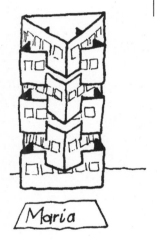

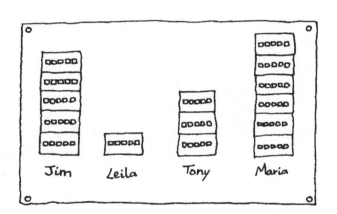

Using the class display and a calculator, the children might like to work out how many people 'live' in each high-rise tower. Tell them that each dot on the faces of the dice counts as one person. The children's answers should end in 5 or 0: for each section there are 5 ⚀, 20 ⚁, 60 ⚂, 80 ⚃, 50 ⚄ and 30 ⚅ . Take this further and make some more three-dimensional model towers. They can be held together with sticky tape. Ask the class to find out how many people there are altogether in these towers by counting all the dots on all three walls.

GAME VARIATIONS

• If the children have difficulty fixing the blocks into the slits, make new sets without slits and rely on the players balancing one block on another. In this case, half the fun of the game is keeping the towers upright! If the game degenerates, with the towers being pushed or blown down 'accidentally' on purpose, change the rules so that the players collect the blocks during the game and only build their towers at the end.

• This is also a good solo game for the child who has a few moments to spare. How high a tower can he build with five throws of the dice? Tell the child to make a number of towers and see which one is the highest. Was it his first, second or third?

HOW TO PLAY DICE TOWERS

For 2 or more players

YOU NEED: some dice tower blocks, a dice and shaker.

❶ Put the tower blocks in the centre of play and sort out the playing order.

❷ Take turns to throw the dice and take a tower block with that dice number on it. If all the tower blocks with that number have gone, then you do not get anything and play passes on to the next player.

❸ Build a tower with your blocks as the game goes on.

❹ When all the blocks have gone from the centre, the game finishes.

❺ Compare your towers.

❻ The one with the highest tower is the winner. The player with the second highest tower is in second place and so on.

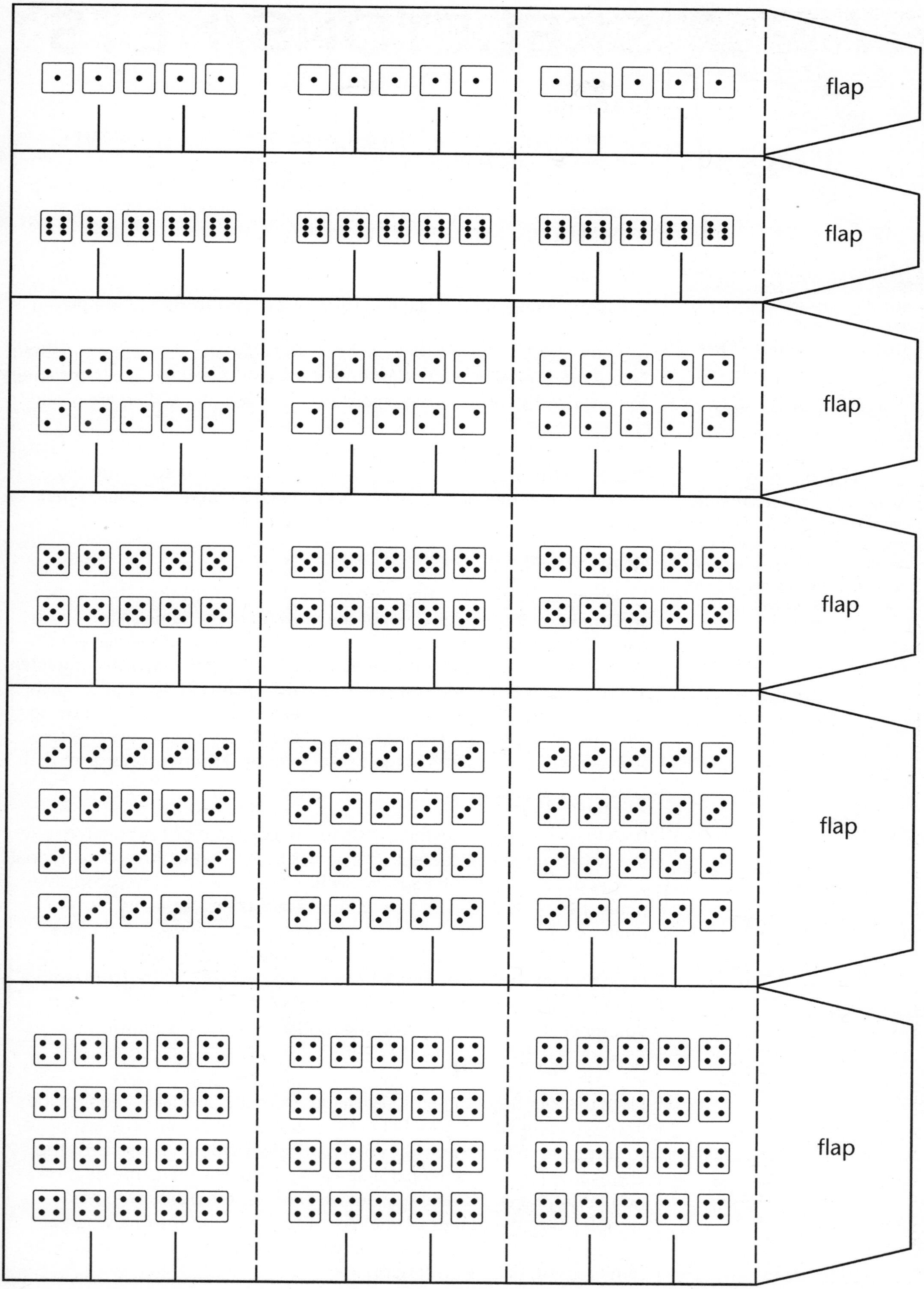

flap

flap

flap

flap

flap

flap

SKELETONS/NETS

TEACHING CONTENT

☆ Examining the structure of a 3-D shape in terms of edges or faces
(SSM: 2a and 2b; RS: A/B)

☆ Recognising 3-D shapes from 2-D representations (SSM: 2a; RS: B/C)

☆ Identifying by name 'cube', 'cuboid' and 'triangular prism'
(SSM: 2c; RS: A/B)

PREPARATION

These two games require different dice and record strips, but are played
in a similar way. Nets for the dice are given on photocopiable pages 120
and 121. Copy the nets on to card, cut them out and stick them together.
Secure the flaps with paper clips until the adhesive is dry. For either game,
you will need an appropriate record strip for each player. Two are given
on each record sheet.

In the 'Skeletons' game, the players overdraw the lines of the skeletal
shapes on the record strip and, therefore, strong coloured felt-tipped
pens are recommended. Each player will need a different coloured pen.
Coloured pencils or crayons are sufficient for the 'Nets' game.

HOW TO PLAY

Skeletons: Each player in turn throws the three-dimensional shapes dice
and draws over *one* edge (line) of the drawing of the same shape on his
record strip. If the shape has all the edges drawn in, or if the player rolls
'Miss a turn', play passes on to the next player. The player who completes
all four shapes first wins. Play continues to find second, third and fourth.
Nets: This game is played as 'Skeletons', except that, instead of drawing
over the edges, faces are coloured in on the shapes on the 'Nets' record
strip according to the roll of the two-dimensional shapes/faces dice.

TEACHER'S ROLE

Both these games require the players to visualise three-dimensional shapes
in a two-dimensional context. The games use the same three-dimensional
shapes as are given in the Special Section (nets given on photocopiable
pages 141–144). If children are unsure, make these shapes as
demonstration models. What shape does the dice show? Point to the
same real shape. Point to the shape on the record strip. Do you have an
edge on that shape that hasn't been drawn over (or, a face that hasn't
been coloured)? Is it the same as this edge (or face) of this shape? Can
you show an edge next to it on the model... and on the drawing?

GAME VARIATION

Place the four three-dimensional shapes from the Special Section (made
from photocopiable pages 141–144) in the centre of play. The first player
to complete the edges or faces of a particular shape on the record strip
claims that three-dimensional shape as a bonus and the game goes on as
normal. At the end, there may be two winners: the player who has
completed all the shapes on the record strip first and the one who has
collected the most bonus three-dimensional shapes. These might be the
same person, but not necessarily.

HOW TO PLAY SKELETONS

For 2 to 4 players

YOU NEED: the three-dimensional shapes (skeletons) dice, a coloured pen and a record strip for each player.

❶ Take turns to throw the dice.

❷ Match the shape on the dice with one on your record strip.

❸ Draw a line along *one* edge of that shape.

❹ If all the edges are already drawn in, play passes on to the next player.

❺ Play also passes on if you throw 'Miss a turn'.

❻ The first player to complete all the edges of all four shapes wins.

HOW TO PLAY NETS

For 2 to 4 players

YOU NEED: the two-dimensional shapes (faces) dice, a coloured crayon or pencil and a record strip for each player.

❶ Take turns to throw the dice.

❷ Match the face on the dice with one on a net on your record strip.

❸ Colour it in.

❹ If all the faces are already coloured, play passes on to the next player.

❺ Play also passes on if you throw 'Miss a turn'.

❻ The first player to complete all the faces on all four nets wins.

RECORD SHEET FOR SKELETONS

Name: _____

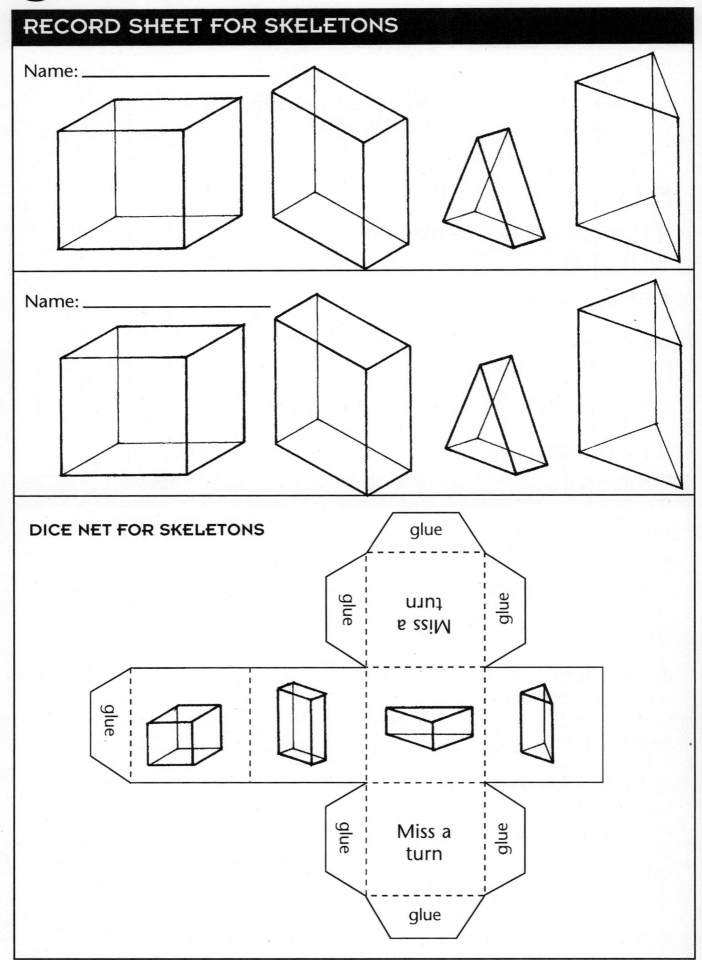

Name: _____

DICE NET FOR SKELETONS

glue

glue

Miss a turn

glue

glue

glue

glue

Miss a turn

glue

glue

RECORD SHEET FOR NETS

Name: _____

Name: _____

DICE NET FOR NETS

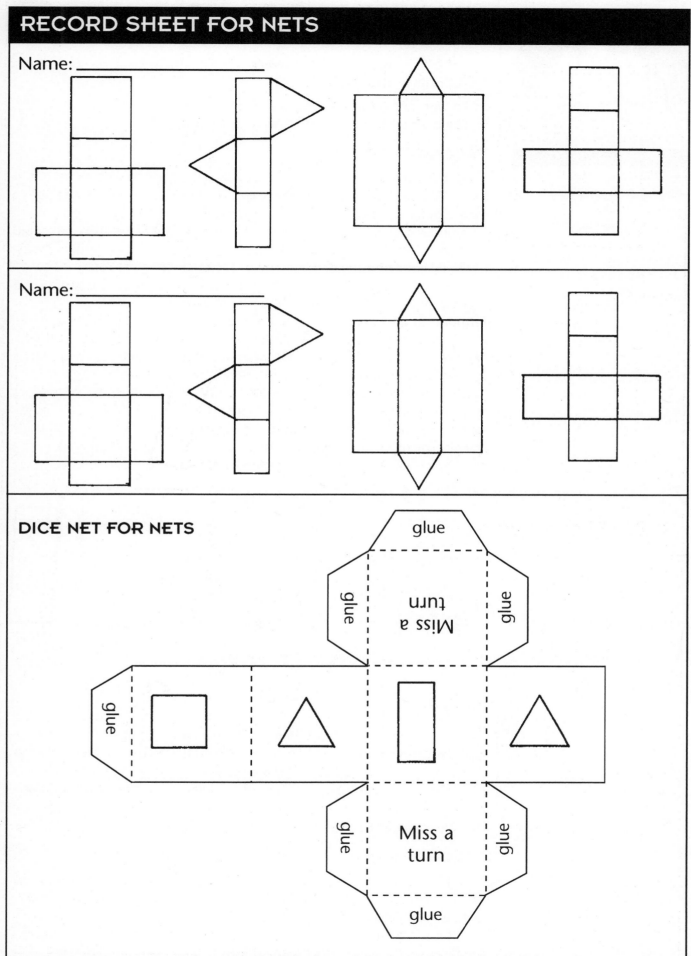

FACE TO FACE

TEACHING CONTENT

☆ Recognising reflective symmetry (SSM: 2c; S: B)
☆ Using a mirror to check symmetry (SSM: 2c; S: B)

PREPARATION

Assembling the game: Copy the face cards directly on to card or mount them. You will need two copies of the sheet in order to make a pack of 48 cards (24 faces). If the cards are to be coloured, use the colours to add differences, for instance the moustache and hair of the second man could be brown, while the hair of the bespectacled man could be yellow. Carefully cut along the dividing line of each pair of cards. You will also need a small child-safe plastic mirror as a checking device. These are available from many classroom equipment suppliers.

Introducing the game: Demonstrate symmetry actively. Let the children make symmetrical patterns with blobs of paint in folded paper. Let them explore which two-dimensional shapes are symmetrical by folding shapes such as squares and circles in half to see if the two halves match.

Develop the discussion to include the human face: If we could fold our faces like a piece of paper to make them symmetrical, which way should we fold them? Identify the features which look roughly the same on both sides of the face: ears, eyes, half the nose and chin, and so on. The children could make their own symmetrical face pictures as follows:

WHAT YOU NEED
PHOTOCOPIABLE PAGES
Face cards sheet 124, 'How to play' sheet 123.
FOR CONSTRUCTION
Card, adhesive, scissors, coloured pens or crayons.
FOR PLAYING
A pack of 48 face cards, a child-safe plastic mirror.

Fold a piece of paper in half. Open it out.

Draw half a face.

Fold the paper outwards and redraw over the lines.

Open out and draw into the marks.

Check the drawing is symmetrical by using a mirror.

HOW TO PLAY

The cards are shuffled and spread out face down in the centre of play. Each player turns over any two cards. If they match, the player keeps them. If they do not match, they are placed face down again and play passes on to the next player. When all the cards have been claimed, the player with the most pairs of cards wins. Throughout the game, face matches can be checked using the mirror.

TEACHER'S ROLE

This game approaches symmetry through a context which is common to all the children – the face. (To take this topic 'out of the classroom', play 'Sym Street' pages 125–127.)

After the game, ask the children to pin-point the differences between the faces on the cards. How many things on each face are different?

HOW TO PLAY FACE TO FACE

For 2 or more players

YOU NEED: the face cards.

❶ Spread out the cards face down and mix them up.

❷ In turn, turn over any two cards.

❸ If they match, you may keep them. If they do not match, place them face down again.

❹ Play goes on to the next player.

❺ When all the cards have been claimed, the player with the most pairs of cards is the winner.

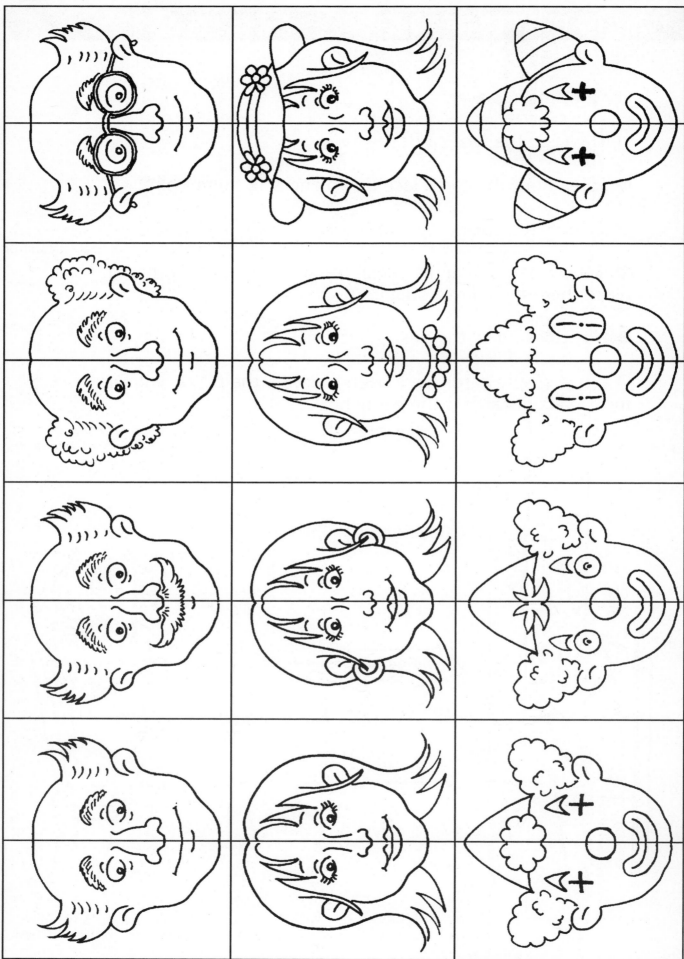

SYM STREET

WHAT YOU NEED

PHOTOCOPIABLE PAGES
*Sym Street cards sheet 127,
'How to play' sheet 126.*

FOR CONSTRUCTION
*Card, scissors, adhesive,
coloured pens or crayons.*

FOR PLAYING
*Sym Street cards, a child-safe
plastic mirror.*

TEACHING CONTENT

☆ Recognising reflective symmetry (SSM: 2c; S: B)
☆ Using a mirror to check symmetry (SSM: 2c; S: B)

PREPARATION

Assembling the game: The cards are best copied directly on to card; otherwise mount them. This is quite a quick game, so one set of cards is sufficient. If the cards are to be coloured, the same colours must be used for each detail of each half. Take care to cut along the thick black lines so that each half is an exact reflection of the other. A child-safe plastic mirror will also be needed.

Introducing the game: Before the game, show the players how the mirror makes a reflection and that it looks similar to the pairs of cards. Use the half pictures on this page to show how the mirror 'completes the picture'.

HOW TO PLAY

This is a game for two players. The cards are shuffled and spread out face down in the centre of play. The first player turns over any card at random and then turns over a second card. If the two match, she puts them together to start in a line: the beginning of Sym Street where everything is symmetrical. If the two cards do not match, they are placed face down again and play passes to the other player. Bit by bit the line of cards will grow from the original pair to make the street. The player who puts the last pair of cards in place is the winner.

TEACHER'S ROLE

If their enthusiasm for 'matching' does not override, you may find that towards the end of the game one, or both, of the players try to pick up non-matching cards deliberately and to remember the positions of the cards which do match as they are revealed, so that she can be the last to put down a matching pair. This would demonstrate that they were thinking about the game in some depth.

Try to ensure that as many of the class as possible have experience of the game before embarking on discussion. Try some four-way symmetry to reinforce the concept. Make two sets of paper photocopies of the cards and ask some of the children to match the pairs and make a street on a board or display panel where everybody can see it. Tell the class that the street is on the banks of a river. What will its reflection look like? Scatter the second set of cards on the table and ask other children to put a reflection in place. What, if anything, is wrong with it? Show how both halves of each picture need to be reflected.

One of the attractions of this game is that the street layout will vary each time the game is played. Paper photocopies of the cards can be stuck on long strips of stiff paper in the same order as the streets in the game to show, for example, 'Jim and Jane's Sym Street' which may well be different to 'Alex and Ann's' . Make a display of these streets. Remind the children, when they are colouring the copies of the cards, to colour both sides of everything the same. They can use the mirror to help them to do this.

HOW TO PLAY SYM STREET

For 2 players

YOU NEED: the Sym Street cards.

❶ Shuffle the cards and spread them out face down in the centre of play.

❷ Take turns to turn over two cards.

❸ If they match you must put them in a line to make part of a street. If they do not match, turn them face down again and let the other players have a go.

❹ The player who puts the last pair in place wins.

TREASURE TREK

TEACHING CONTENT

☆ Using right angles as a measure of turn (SSM: 3b; PM: B)
☆ Recognising right angles (SSM: 3b; PM: B)
☆ Using the four points of the compass (PM: B)

PREPARATION

Assembling the game: This game can be played to explore right angles or the points of the compass. Dice nets are provided for both versions. Assemble the chosen net, supporting the dice by filling it with crumpled paper. You may wish to mount the A3 colour pull-out board for this game on to card and laminate it. Each player will need four counters, or coins, and a pirate playing piece. Colour the pirates to match the four 'colour' corners of the board. The counters do not have to be the same colours as the pirates.
Introducing the game: Talk about pirates. Explain how the the talkative parrot will tell them where the treasure map is hidden. The map shows where the key and treasure chest are and, of course, the key must be found to open the chest. Discuss the faces of the chosen dice and link them to the squares on the game board. Explain how the small black arrow on the dice always points to the top of the map (north) and is drawn also on every square. The white arrow points the direction in which to go.

HOW TO PLAY

This is a game for two to four 'pirates'. Each player puts her pirate playing piece on the same coloured 'pirate' picture square. This indicates the colour of the items for which the player is aiming. In turn, each player throws the dice and moves his pirate in a straight line in the direction shown on the dice until it reaches and stops at the next available picture square. If the square is the same colour as the pirate, the player can put a counter on the same picture in his colour corner. If the picture square and the pirate do not match, nothing happens. If 'Free choice' is thrown, the player can pick any direction in which to move. If a pirate is already occupying the next picture square, or if the move would take the pirate off the board into 'shark-infested seas', or if 'Miss this turn' is thrown, the player cannot move. The first player to 'collect' all the four items wins.

TEACHER'S ROLE

After the game, ask the children how many turns each player made. They will have forgotten! So tell them to play the game again, but show them how to make a tally of each turn. Help them to count the number of turns/right angles at the end. How many complete turns did they make? (Every four quarters equals one complete turn.) This is not recommended for compass turns as it is hard for the children to equate so many east or so many west with complete compasses, but you could explain that turning east is the same as one right-angle turn and so on.

GAME VARIATION

Extend the game by requiring the children to collect the items in the same sequence as in the story: parrot first, map second and so on. (This is the same order as the pictures are given in the colour corners.)

Tally of Right Angles

⌐	✓✓✓	3
╤	✓	2
╪	✓✓	6
▦	✓✓✓	12
		23÷4

I turned 23 right angles enough for 5 full turns and 3 left over

HOW TO PLAY TREASURE TREK

For 2 to 4 players

YOU NEED: the A3 colour game board, a right-angles or compass points dice, a shaker, a pirate playing piece and four counters or coins for each player.

❶ Put your pirate on the same coloured pirate picture square on the board.

❷ In turn, throw the dice and move in the direction shown to the next available picture square.

❸ If the colour of the picture square and your pirate match, put a counter on the same picture in your colour corner. If they do not match just wait on this square until your next go.

❹ You cannot move:

IF the next picture square has another pirate on it;

IF your move would take you off the island into the shark-infested seas without reaching a picture square;

IF you throw 'Miss this turn'.

❺ If you throw 'Free choice', you can choose which direction to move in to the next picture square.

❻ The first player to put a counter on all four of his or her items – parrot, map, key and treasure chest – is the winner.

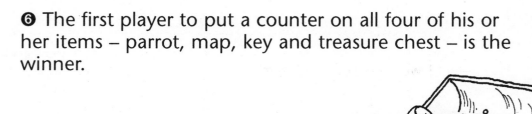

TREASURE TREK DICE NETS AND PLAYING PIECES

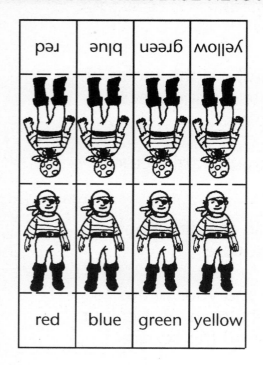

red	blue	green	yellow

Stick and hold with a paper clip until the adhesive is dry.

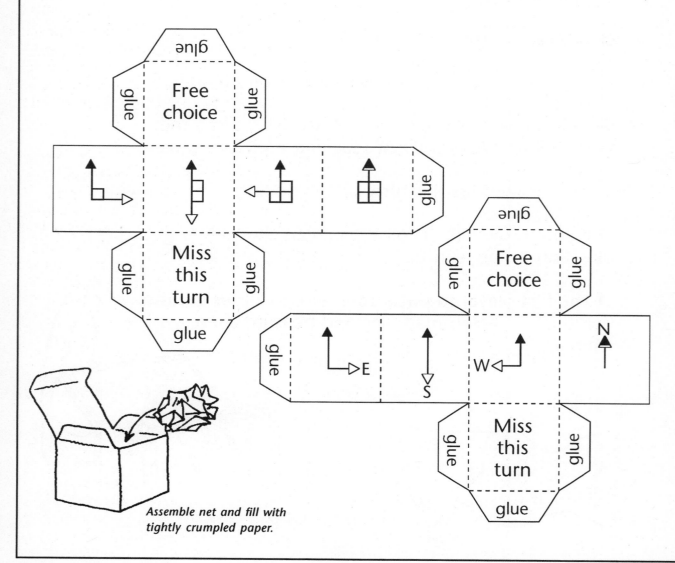

Assemble net and fill with tightly crumpled paper.

PHOTOCOPIABLE PAGES
'How to play' sheet with measures dice 132.

FOR CONSTRUCTION
Card, scissors, adhesive, paper clips, tissue paper.

FOR PLAYING
'Measure, fill, weigh' A3 colour pull-out game board, the 'measures' dice and shaker, 'How to play' sheet, a counter for each player.

MEASURE, FILL, WEIGH

TEACHING CONTENT

☆ Placing measuring instruments in the correct contexts (SSM: 1c; ME: A)
☆ Choosing appropriate measuring instruments (N: 4b; ME: A)

PREPARATION

Assembling the game: You will need the A3 colour pull-out game board for this game which you may wish to mount on to thick card and laminate. Copy the measures dice net on to card and assemble it. Hold it together with paper clips until the adhesive is dry, then fill it tightly with crumpled paper. Alternatively, stick the pairs of measures pictures opposite each other on a play brick. Each player will need a different coloured counter.

Introducing the game: Ensure that the children know the different measurement words, both written and verbally. Highlight examples of weighing, filling and measuring from class activities and outside school.

HOW TO PLAY

This is a game for two or more players. To start, each player must throw the face of the dice which matches the first picture on the board – the tape measure to 'Measure the chalkboard'. To move along the board from square to square, the right measuring instrument to measure, fill or weigh the item shown has to be thrown. The player who gets to 'Weigh three apples' and throws the rocker balance first is the winner.

TEACHER'S ROLE

This game is based on the main physical operations of measurement – weighing, filling and measuring length. The players have to recognise which method is best suited for a particular task. The solutions are generally clear, but there is reinforcement of measurement language throughout, and there are one or two puzzlers, such as whether a jug is suitable for filling something with sand. It is not the conventional use of a jug, but as the dice offers only a tape and a balance as alternatives, it is the best choice. Similarly, although the four main words of length (height, length, width and depth) are introduced, it is not essential to know them to play the game, as the choices are limited. During the game, correct wrong use of these words. At an opportune moment, use the word 'measure' instead of 'fill' or 'weigh'. Point out that 'measure' can be applied to all the activities, not just those to do with length. Observe which players recognise which method is best suited for a particular task.

GAME VARIATION

If the game appears to be too easy for the group, alter the dice to include some *inappropriate* measuring instruments, for instance a clock and a trundle wheel (not ideal for any of the measuring activities shown), and a shovel (possibly allowable for filling the plant pot and the box of sand). If these are thrown, the throw is wasted and play passes on to the next player. Always discuss the suitability of the measuring instrument thrown.

HOW TO PLAY MEASURE, FILL, WEIGH

For 2 or more players

YOU WILL NEED: the game board, the 'measures' dice and shaker, a different coloured counter for each player.

❶ To move around the board you must throw the face of the dice which matches the next picture.

So: to start a tape measure has to be thrown.

❷ Move from square to square in the directions of the arrows. There can be more than one counter on a square.

❸ The first player to get to 'Weigh three apples' and throws the balance wins.

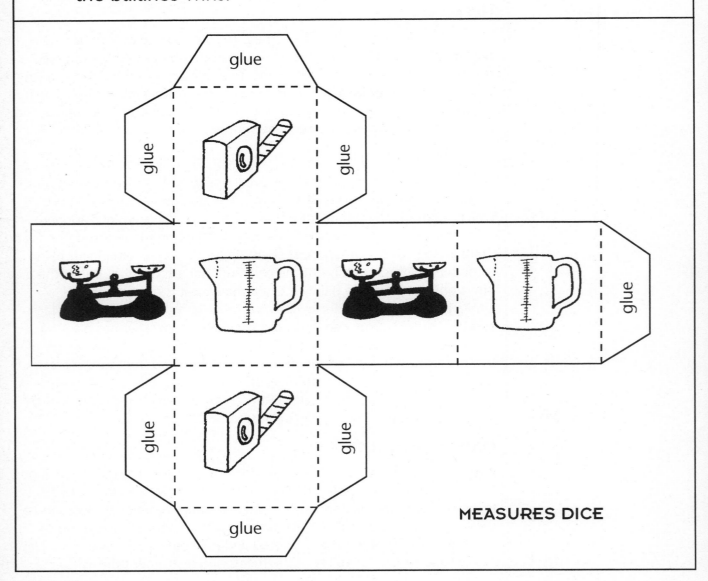

MEASURES DICE

MATHS
GAMES

KEY STAGE
ONE
1

Special section

ABOUT THIS SECTION

Two aspects of two- and three-dimensional shape are emphasised in both the National Curriculum and the Scottish 5–14 Guidelines: the importance of children being able to make common shapes and models as part of the process of classification of shapes (SSM: 2b [both KS1 and KS2]; RS: A, B, D and E), and the recognition of the geometrical features of shapes such as faces, edges, sides, angles, corners and vertices (SSM: 2c [KS1] and 2b [KS2]; RS: A, B and D).

Most commercially-available shapes are adequate, but do not help very much with the process of identifying some of these features. Presented with a one-colour three-dimensional shape, for instance, a child may have difficulty distinguishing one face of it from another. The shapes in this Special Section make this process a little easier by highlighting certain characteristics, namely sides (two-dimensional shapes), edges (three-dimensional shapes), angles (a curve in each corner), right angles (a square 'box' in each corner) and planes and faces (by human faces).

Remember that the photocopies can be altered to emphasise just one of each characteristic, if so desired. For example, you may wish to have a cube showing only the edges, in which case delete the faces and angles so that the cube would have only the 12 edges marked.

This Special Section contains cards showing a range of two-dimensional shapes and the nets for four three-dimensional shapes: a cube, a cuboid and two triangular prisms.

TWO-DIMENSIONAL SHAPES CARDS

The 12 shapes chosen for these cards cover most of the day-to-day two-dimensional shapes you may need, including the parallelogram and rhombus. They are all mentioned in either or both of the National Curriculum and the Scottish 5–14 Guidelines. Do not be too afraid of introducing the proper names. If the children absorb them, so much the better. If not, there is little harm in them being confronted by the real names for the shapes.

The cards are best copied directly on to card. If you have to mount them, use medium-thin card and ensure that the edges are stuck down well. If they are to be coloured, leave the main body of the cards white and colour only the properties of the shapes; that is, the angles, the edges and the faces. Keep to one colour for the edges and one for the angles, but colour the faces to represent a range of ethnic backgrounds. The shape cards have been designed to be 'user-friendly', each having a smiling face on it. This is not merely decoration. The face provides a word association with 'surface' or 'face' meaning 'a flat plane', which is of particular value when investigating the properties of three-dimensional shapes. The straight sides of the shapes on the cards are emphasised by a decorative wavy edge and the angles are drawn either as a square for right angles or as a curved corner for all other angles. For older or more-able children, these angles could be differentiated into obtuse and acute angles by writing a tiny 'o' or 'a' inside them or by a colour code.

The cards can be used in several of the games in this book (see pages 15, 16, 19, 22 and 72), as well as being a useful resource in their own right. Further specific game ideas are given below. Besides this, they are so relatively cheap that the children can have a set per group table, or even a set each. Then they can be quickly taken out for some revision of the properties of shapes in any spare minute: Show me a shape with three sides, ...with four angles, ...with four right angles, ...with one side and no angles. This last example is for the semicircle. Strictly speaking the straight edge can be drawn as two sides meeting at the centre with a double right angle or 180° angle. It has not been drawn as such here because it might cause confusion, but if it is thought that the children will understand this, amend the semicircle to show its 'hidden' properties.

The children should be encouraged to see the two-dimensional flat shapes as parts of the three-dimensional solid shapes. Thus, the child may see the two-dimensional square replicated, so to speak, on the surfaces of the cube and so on. Instead of being used as cards, the shapes can be cut out and used to build other shapes to emphasise this property. For instance, a cube could be constructed from six squares held in place with sticky tape. To facilitate this, it is suggested that you make an A4 master sheet, cut and pasted from copies of each card; so there could be a master sheet of squares, another of rectangles and so on.

TWO-DIMENSIONAL SHAPES CARD GAMES

The two-dimensional shapes cards can be used for a variety of simple card games acquainting the children with the shapes. Reduce and cut and paste them on to an A4 master sheet. This is best copied directly on to card. You will need four copies (48 cards) for a good set of cards.

Snap

This game for two players is an old favourite, if a trifle noisy. The cards are shuffled and placed in a pack face down. Each player turns over the top card and puts it, face up, on an adjoining stack. If that card matches the one underneath, both players call out 'SNAP'. The first one to do so wins all the cards. If a wrong call is made, play goes on, but the player who called out incorrectly cannot call out again until the other player has had a successful call. Play should go on until only one player has all the cards, but this can be quite time consuming, so if you decide to call an end to the proceedings, the player with the most cards wins.

Spread

Yet another old favourite, this is usually a game for two to four players. The cards are spread out face down in the centre of the table and shuffled around until everyone is satisfied that no one knows where any particular shape is located. The first player turns over two cards. If they match, he can keep them. If they do not match, he turns them face down again. The next player then turns over any two cards, one at a time. Again, if they match, they are kept; if not, they are turned face down again. The game is one of memorising where similar shapes are positioned and learning to turn over the second card strategically, either trying a card that has been already turned and you think might match or trying a completely new card. When all the cards have been claimed the player with the most pairs wins.

Right angles

For this game, the rules of 'Snap' or 'Spread' apply, but the objective is to match only shapes with right angles. For example, 'Snap' could be applied to a square and a quadrant (a quarter circle) as they both have right angles. A further refinement could be to allow 'Snap' only for shapes with the same *number* of right angles; for example, a square and a rectangle, or a quadrant and a right-angled triangle.

Alternatively, similar objectives could be applied to 'Spread.'

The Different Family

This is a game for at least three players. Each player starts with four cards. The rest are placed in a pack face down. In turn, the players take the top card and either lay it face up in a discard stack alongside the main pack or exchange it for one of the cards in their hand, which in turn is put on the discard stack. The players can choose also to take the top discard stack card instead and exchange it for one in their hands. The object of the game is to get a 'family' of four completely different shapes, for example a circle, a triangle, a hexagon and a square. The players put down their four cards when they think they have such a family. If any other player can find a similarity between the shapes – the same number of sides, or right angles in two of the shapes, for example – the hand is rejected and the player takes up her hand again and misses a go. The first player to put down a hand of four completely different shapes is the winner.

THREE-DIMENSIONAL SHAPES NETS

These four shapes are all relevant to the content of the National Curriculum and the Scottish 5–14 Guidelines. They were chosen because they have straight edges and flat faces. Two of the shapes are cuboids, that is, they are shaped similarly to a cube, but can have rectangular faces, and two are prisms, that is, they have two equal faces separated by same-sized rectangular faces. Like their two-dimensional counterparts, the edges are decorated and the angles are also drawn in as curves or squares. The decorated edges emphasise the meeting of the flat surfaces, while corners are shown as a meeting of angles. However, for these shapes, the faces drawn on take on more significance. For two-dimensional shapes, it is apparent that there is only one plane face on each shape. However, for three-dimensional shapes, there are a varying number of faces beaming back at their users, emphasising the relationships between two- and three-dimensional shapes.

While they are central to some of the games in the text (see pages 19, 22, 60, 86 and 118), these three-dimensional shapes can be used for all sorts of exploratory activities. But, perhaps, one of their most important roles would be to be in a tray or box readily available for the class to look at and handle at any time.

CHILDREN'S CONSTRUCTION OF THE THREE-DIMENSIONAL SHAPES

It may be possible for the children to make some three-dimensional shapes themselves. This is a valid activity in its own right. Making three-dimensional shapes of increasing complexity with greater accuracy is an objective of both the National Curriculum and the Scottish 5–14 Guidelines. If the children in the class are too young to assemble the shapes, they could be made by a parents' group or by older children.

A photocopiable sheet (page 140) has been provided to direct the children how to make the shapes. It is best if each stage can be carried out separately. Long intervals between gluing each part are *essential* to allow the adhesive used to dry thoroughly and to avoid parts which have already been assembled inadvertently coming unstuck. The children should not be expected to glue and hold together more than one part at a time. Link the construction to some other model-making activity so that the stages can be spaced out.

Each shape is assembled in the same way. As with the two-dimensional shapes cards, each net is best copied directly on to card. Colour the faces, edges and angles, preferably with felt-tipped pens, as described on page 134 for the shape cards. Let the ink dry thoroughly before cutting out the net. Write the name of the child constructing the shape on the inside of the net *now* (or ask the child to write it).

Make all the folds in advance so that the shape can be assembled easily. Put glue on to flap 1 of the main structure. Hold it in place with paper clips at each end and then leave it to dry completely.

Press down flaps 2 in a right angle at one end of the shape, put adhesive on the flaps and then press up the square/triangular end on to the glued flaps. Turn the shape on to the newly glued face and press down the flaps from inside. Put some small weights, such as marbles, into the shape to hold the flaps in place until they are dry.

When the first flaps are dry, take out the weights and fill the shape with crumpled paper to give added support. (If the shape is to be used for '3-D hoopla', pages 60–63, put in an appropriately-shaped thin piece of Plasticine to cover the inside of the base of the shape as a weight.)

Finally, fold in flaps 3 in a right angle, put adhesive on to them and fold on the square/triangular top. Run your fingers round the edge of the top to check that the flaps are in firm contact. They can be held in place with a light weight, but be careful not to get any adhesive between the top of the shape and the weight. Again let the adhesive dry thoroughly.

HOW TO CONSTRUCT A 3-D SHAPE

❶ Colour in the faces, edges and angles.

❷ Cut out the net. Fold all the flaps.

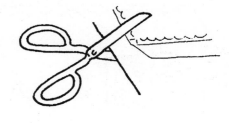

❸ Write your name on the back of one of the end flaps.

❹ Bend in and glue flap 1. Hold it in place with paper clips. Let it dry!

❺ Bend in and glue flaps 2. Press the face on to the flaps. Turn the shape upside down and press the flaps from inside. You may like to put some marbles inside to hold the flaps in place. Let the flaps dry!

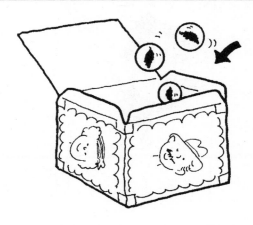

❻ Take out the marbles. Fill the shape with crumpled paper.

❼ Bend in and glue flaps 3. Press the top of the shape on to the flaps. Hold it down with a small weight until it is dry.

CUBE

CUBOID

SMALL TRIANGULAR PRISM

LONG TRIANGULAR PRISM

LONG TRIANGULAR PRISM